The Longest Furrow Volume 1

By Frederick Charles Waterfall (Owd Fred)

First Published July 2009
© Fred Waterfall Publications (Countryman)
8.10.2013
Email — mail@fcwaterfall.co.uk

Dedicated to the memory of our son
Matthew

All money raised from the sale of these books goes to
Headways North Staffs.
The head injuries' charity

Introduction.

An open letter of introduction about my book to an old school friend who I spoke to a few years ago, recalling all the old school mates of that time, and the old folk who lived in the village.

22/11/08

Dear Mrs G———-n,

A lot of what I have written is quite selfishly about myself and my family and how we grew up in the forties and fifties, but it's only people of our age can relate to those hard times, and about school life. As a pupil at Seighford school yourself you remember the different teachers, each one having their own quirky ways, Miss Pye who rode her bicycle from Doxey every morning, and had two groups or ages of children to cope with, and the big blazing open fire in each class room.

Miss or was it Mrs Hetherington who died, I was in the infants then, Miss Worthington who came to school in her little Morris car, I remember what a big jaw she had. Mr Hall, he came in a car from Cannock and was often late for assembly, when he had got to collect and bring some of his father's builder gang to work at Seighford each morning, they were then just building the first ten council houses in the village.

As on any momentous occasion you can remember where you were and what you were doing when a certain thing happened, and you do not forget it, such was the occasion when old Mrs Steel emptied her gazunder out of the bedroom window, to dissuade children from playing anywhere near her rooms and windows. Remember Mrs Appleby the caretaker who had to light the fires every morning and stoke the big boiler with coal to heat the water pipes, also had to clean the toilets, any solids content went into the garden, no wonder the soil was so black and rich. Us lads had an open to the sky latrines, and had to pee into a gully that was along the boundary wall to Mr Appleby's garden, I remember at break time there could be up to six of us who all trying our best to pee over the wall and laughed about his cabbage and sprouts on the other side that benefitted.

The school bus came from Derrington, a very posh Greatrix tour coach, we called it the "Derrybobs" bus the Rawsthorne lads came on that as did the Turner lads from Aston Hall, when they moved it was Atkins sisters lived there, Mousey G and Dennis C from along Aston Cottages. In the village it was nearly all lads, four Frost lads, four of us Waterfall's, three of Reg Flowers lads, three Appleby lads next to the school and two of Albert Hine lads. The vicars son Chad was an only lad (He did have a sister) and a bit older than our group but we nearly hung him one day when we were trying to climb "Everest", it was when Everest had just been conquered for the first time.

We had a rope over one of Bill Appleby's foul pens (Everest) pulling each other up from the far side, the one being pulled and three or four of us doing the pulling, it worked okay until Chad got the rope round his neck and we managed to just get him off the ground and could not get him any further, on looking round the pen we let him go, he had a very red rope burn round his neck for days and I swear he was a bit taller.

It's always nice to look back on those days, and remember thing that happened and the people and characters of the village and how they lived.

Hope you enjoy the book and thank you for your donation for our charity, "Head Injuries".

Thanks again,

Fred Waterfall

Table of Contents

Chapter
1 I first Started to try my hand
2 Onslow Park
3 The Weather Forecast by Owd Fred's Mother
4 Bit long in the Tooth
5 Village Craftsmen
6 You may like to see my Tractors
7 This is the Story of my Operation
8 Two ,ore of my Tractors
9 Father Grew Sugar Beet
10 The Long Harvest (1938-2008)
11 Father always kept Ayrshire Cows
12 Farm as if you'll Farm for Ever
13 Feathers floating Round the Light
14 "Trotters"
15 The Village Wheelwright and his Family
16 Verse to the Wheelwrights Shop
17 Grandma's best Strong Float
18 To farming College I was Sent
19 Norfolk Four Coarse Rotation
20 The Old Gypsy was about to "Skin Me"
21 Long Toe nails like claws to Grip on the Perch
22 The Great escape "Getting out of me Chair"
23 Climate Change the hot Topic
24 Exploring the Bacon Pits (1948)
25 Mother always Worked so hard
26 Remember mother Lighting the Kitchen Fire
27 The Cows have got a Leader
28 Old Characters of the Village
29 Mother's Christmas Puddings
30 Corn (wheat) Harvest 1940's
31 I Remember Mothers Christmas Cakes
32 Animals in our Lives

Our Village, top left is The Beeches Farm where we were brought up above left of the church tower is Church Farm, Yews Farm bottom left with the white building.

Chapter 1

I first started to try my Hand

This is a record of my life, far from complete and about when I first started to try my hand at writing at the age of 70.

The poems, verses and tales are from my own life experiences, centered round my home, the farm and the village. About all the characters that lived and worked in the village when I was growing up having lived here all my life.

Born at Brook House Farm, Aston Doxey, reared from the age of four at Beeches Farm Seighford, Farmed at Church Farm from the age of twenty one to the age of forty, then moved to The Yews Farm, up to present day. All within the Parish of Seighford no more than a mile and half apart.

Memory is a fickle thing for me, and looking back years ago it seems most clear, but then there is no one going to challenge what you claim to know. Details of the most irrelevant things come to mind, and always after you should have remembered, and too dam late to tell.

Just Got Over Retiring Age

I've just got over retiring age,
and only now put pen to page,
And now I'm getting past my prime,
Thing appear all in rhyme,

Following a train of thought,
It must be a bug that I've caught,
On looking back all through my life,
how lucky I've been to have good wife,

She generally sorts out all my bugs,
As well as order all the drugs,
Cuts my hair and wash my cloths,
Boots I wash down with a hose,
Food it's bought with so much care,
Low salt and sugar be aware,
Meal are always at a regular time,
This I'm used to whole my lifetime,

Get up early every morning, when
Most folks they are still a snoring,
When cows I milked got up five thirty,
In for breakfast hands were dirty,
Not done this for twenty years,
But this old habit never blears,
A couple of hours of time and thought,
Before breakfast rhymes to mind are brought.

———

Looking Back them Years Ago

    This is a tale of when we started school and growing up, and when we were left in the evening for the first time. Father always made our toys and were almost inevitably tractors with trailers. When father made a toy it was made to last and usually carve out of a block of oak.

Looking Back them Years Ago (1940's)

Looking back them years ago,
when we were little boys,
We bumped our knees and elbows,
and father made us toys,
Played around the farmyard,
in and out the sheds,
Testing all the puddles,
thick mud into the house it treads.

When at first we started school,
father trimmed our hair,
Combed and washed with new cap,
new shoes without compare,
Short trousers and new jacket,
a satchel on our back,
We all went there to study,
but often got a smack.

Times tables chanted every morning,
and the alphabet,
Till we knew them off by heart,
of this I've no regret,
Isn't till you leave school,
that you realize,
How useful school and education,
help to make us wise.

Father showed us all his skills,
from very early age,
Studied Farmers Weekly,
read almost every page,
The pictures they were mainly,
of inter-est to us,
News and reports on prices,
what a blooming fuss.

We also had the Beano,
a comic for us kids,
Dandy and the Eagle,
must have cost dad quid's,
Him he had his farmers weekly,
it must be only fare,
Mother had a knitting book,
for inspiration n' flare.

It must have taken fifteen years,
till we felt grown up,
Left alone at home at night,
parents meeting as a group,
In fact it was a whist drive
every Friday night,
We supposed to be in bed,
but sometimes had a fright.

An owl it hooted in bright moonlight,
scared us all to death,
Door that blew in wind,
with fright we nearly lost our breath,
Scooted up the stairs so fast,
and under the bedclothes dove,
In darkness we were frightened,
it was for courage that we strove.

On hearing the back door open,
it was never locked,
Foot steps in the kitchen,
bedroom door we chocked,
Then we heard mothers
Coo-eee, relieved to hear her call,
Have you missed me duckies?
we bloomin have an all.

So our sheltered life was over,
sometimes fended for ourselves,
Mother learned us basic cooking,
as long as plenty on the shelves,

One at a time we left home,
with basic thing that we were taught,
This knowledge we're to build on,
foundations life not bought.

Father's Cattle

In the mid 1950's vets were recommending worming young stock with a new product called phenothiazine. This was a powder and had to be mixed with water and a pint or so was pour down their throats (drenched)

To catch the young stock that needed worming, we used to drive them into a loose box or stable or the small cow shed that only held six cows, this meant that they were tight and could not run away, two of us lads went in among them and the bottles of drench would be handed to us. I don't think crushes had been invented then, but father later made one for himself out of oak, and the blacksmith made some straps of iron to brace it all together.

I Remember Father's Cattle

I remember father counting,
cattle each and every day,
He counts and looks at every one,
to see they're all OK,
Now one day he sees one cough,
and then it was another.
If we don't do something quickly,
we'll be in a bit of bother.

So off down he goes to get,
some wormer in a rush,
And back he comes and reads
the label, says get them in a crush,
No crush have we, but four strong lads,
we'll get them in a stable,
Mix water and green powder in
a bucket, put it on the table.

Four long neck bottles we did find,
for dosing all the cattle,
Phenothiozine, it's called,
and keep it stirred or it will settle,
The pop had gone as we made sure;
we loved the fizzy taste,
One pint and half was dose that's needed,
over dose was waste.

Pint ladle and a funnel now,
into the bottled it was measured,
Us lads went in among the stock,
as tightly they were gathered,
The bottles we did pass to one,
who had ones chin held high,
Uptip the med-sin to back of throat,
do not look down or ni.

The cow that coughs, coughs both ends,
chuck it back they try,
Its just a waste as we were told,
but hits you in the eye,
Soon learn to leave it quickly,
as soon as we could shift,
As dosing cattle get their own back,
now who's being thrift.

We often wondered why we lads,
had grown so big and strong,
When other lads around us,
were only lean and long,
Put it down to fresh air,
and read farmers weekly magazine,
But all the time it wasn't,
twas Phenothiazine.

Now a story or two about Mother

In this one where we refer to "steam coal" it was coal that was rolled off the tender of a steam engine, as the main railway line ran through our distant fields.

Most men were in the home guard and father got to know this engine driver from there, he often exchanged a half a pig for no end of coal. He would slow his engine and his fireman would go up top would roll big lumps off as fast as he could, when father counted his cattle in a mornings he would take a cart with him and bring back the coal, all this happened at a set time each morning for over a week, or until he had got enough.

I don't know how mother came to have such a strong grip, but if she caught a hold of you for some reason, there was no hope of getting away, perhaps it was the hand milking in her younger days that gave her that grip, I remember some old cows were very hard to milk, it seems to have been bred out of them nowadays along with the bad feet and curled up toes and pendulous udders.

Mother had a Grip like Iron

When mother was young had help,
around the family farm,
Milking cows by hand,
strengthened sinews in her arms,
Her hand were still ladies hands,
no bulky muscle show,
Belied the strength built into them,
beyond you'd ever know.

Mother had a grip like iron,
nothing failed her grip,
Screw lids on jars and bottles,
give it me she'd quip,
The grip she had to skin a rabbit,
or ring an old hen's neck,
Crush a grape; she'd crush a walnut,
power she'd got by heck.

By the coal ruck was her hammer,
there to break the coal,
Coal it came in big lumps,
from steam loco it was bowled,
For coal alone the big lump hammer,
it was there reduce,
Best steam coal was hard and bright,
cracked it down for use.

When were young she'd lace our boots,
bow she'd pull real tight,
They never came undone all day,
right into the night,
Sewing did with button thread,
no tear came open again,
And buttons only came off once,
thread she used times ten.

With age her hands were not so
nimble, feel it gradually went,
Knitting she'd done all her life,
on wool she no more spent,
Skin n' nails were without blemish,
soft and pink they were,
On grip she never lost her strength
she was the best mum ever.

When she sat down in the evening, mother would pick up her knitting, she could knit without looking and when we had our first television she could watch and knit at the same time. Jumpers hats gloves scarves socks she always had a good stock of wool. There seemed to be two stock colours, grey and fawn, other colours were bought for a specific jumper or sweater. When the need arose she would be darning socks, nowadays they get thrown and a new pair bought. She liked to experiment with new patterns which she gleaned from her magazine, but mostly she only did the patterns up the front where it would be seen, then she could "bomb" on with the back and would produce a jumper in a week.

Mothers Weekly Magazine

Mother had weekly magazine,
knitting patterns every week,
These she used to knit up the fronts,
of our jumpers so to speak,
Some were cable some were ribbed,
some were chequered squares,
Some were bobbles in a lump,
couldn't buy anything that compares.

The wool she bought was in skeins,
a dozen at a time,
This she got us to hold while she
wound into balls like twine,
We held our hands out at full stretch,
while she wound full tilt,
Arms would ache on the second one,
then our arms would wilt.

Brother next in line was asked,
turns we had to take,
Wool was grey, or fawn, or blue,
for what she'd got to make,
Socks she knit one every night,
jumpers took over a week,
Stitch the front and back together,
sleeves to the arm holes tweak.

Started with the welt,
the grippe bit round the waist,
Tested it on, one who it's for,
half way round our hips she placed,
On up to the armpits,
try it for length again,
Then the neck onto the shoulder,
it was a blooming pain.

Next the socks they're mostly grey,
started top welt round,
These were pulled up to our knee,
and turned the top bit down,
Knit on down to the heel,
measured it on our legs,
Three needles used on this job,
pulled them on like stuck out pegs.

Heels we always wore out first,
    so in with the wool she knit,
Strong button thread alongside the
    wool, patterns this wasn't writ,
So when they did get bare and thin,
    she darned them time agen,
Then they were called our working
    socks, for us working men.

Sometimes when jumpers,
    got wore out up the front,
She would unpick the seams,
    and rewind a whole segment,
Then would knit again, into
    little gloves or woolly hat,
In winter balaclava, or scarves
    on many things she'd tat.

When we were young she'd knit and knit,
    no woollies bought at all,
As we left home she knit again,
    next generation when they're small,
Knit up to her seventies,
    when finger would not flex no more,
Big blow it was, she knit by feel,
    for old age yet, there is no cure.

Let no one ever come to you without leaving a bit happier.
    Mother Teresa (1910 – 1997)

Chapter 2

Onslow Park

It's a vintage tractor show with a working area demonstrating the old tractors and ploughs and other ground working implements. In the working area there will be a big plough, a Ransomes Hexatrac five furrow pulled by a crawler driven by Roy.

I bought this plough five years ago out of a Tractor & Machinery magazine, it had been parked up when reversible ploughs came in and it formed the foundation of a huge scrap ruck, where it stayed for over 40years. I rang up about it and was told it could not be seen until it had been uncovered and the scrap on top of it sold. He took my number as he did with six other people, and I never heard from him at all, he had lost all the phone numbers, and I was the first to ring him up, and he described what it was and its condition. I bought it over the phone not seen and arranged transport home. I spent nearly a year on loosening up it joints and replaced the mole boards discs and skims then painted it to match my County Crawler

Found a Ramsomes Hexatrac

Found a Ramsomes Hexatrac,
five furrows in a row,
Did have six but one got lost,
in a scrap ruck well below,
It came from south coast Lewes,
overlooks the channel,
Only used a few years when,
mounted ploughs became its rival.

Pulled out the field and parked,
for forty years or more,
Years of scrap iron piled on top,
red coat of rust it wore,
Advertised in magazine,
list of numbers he had got,
But nere could see the plough,
still beneath its iron plot.

Took a couple of months until,
it was unearthed for to see,
Then lost the numbers he had got,
then got a call from me.
Bought it o'r the phone that night,
arranged a haulage home,
Robo's wagons go his way,
along the south coast roam.

Picked it up in mid-week,
three days touring it did get,
All round London city touted,
not even getting wet,
Arrived at Robo's Seighford depot,
late on Satdee morning,
Amazed to see the size and weight,
for care and oil its calling.

All the joints and screw threads seized,
caster wheel was solid,
The poor owd plough found good
home, soaked with diesel rapid,
Gradually it loosened up,
all the joints and handles turned,
Fitted brand new mole boards,
points n discs n skims it earned.

Ready now the field to go,
and set the furrows up,
So many furrows to adjust,
for days it was no letup,
Eventually it all was set,
a working weekend booked,
This rusty hulk of iron now,
a plough again it looked.

A dazzle of shinny metal now,
beneath its rusty frame,
To turn a crooked furrow,
it's the ploughman you must blame,
It turns them good and even,
and covers a lot of ground,
To learn to start and finish now,
a must for me I'm bound.

Ready now for coat of paint,
to match the County Crawler,
Light blue frame and wheels of
orange, it really looks a mauler,
But on light land takes it easily,
a real good matching pair,
To find another plough like this,
there's nothing to compare.

For five years I have had the set,
lot of work and pleasure had,
Its heavy to load and get about,
no longer am I a lad,
Time to find a new home,
not too far so I can go and see,
Them still working how they
used to,all still working ably.

This is my County Crawler I did up to pull the plough, here it is working at home. I have taken it to about five or six ploughing matches each year and it makes an excellent job. The whole outfit got to be a maul for me to load and unload, so I sold it to a younger chap

Roy from Chetton Bridgnorth in Shropshire about thirty miles away. It is Roy who is taking it to the Onslow Park Vintage Weekend in the working area. Now I've got a Fordson E27N with a three furrow Fordson Elite plough and a matching furrow press for our local working weekends and a two furrow hydraulic Ford Ransome two furrow to go to ploughing matches with.

Invention is the mother of necessity
Thorstein Veblem

Chapter 3

The Weather Forecast by Owd Fred's Mother

Our mother always "did" the weather for all the family, she could give a "forecast" based on what stage the phase of the moon was at, and watching the house barometer closely. Even into her eighties we could contact her and the first thing was, the weather, and was advised when to start hay making or combining and so on, and the prospects for the following week. From what I learned from her, the weather will set a trend in the first few days of the new moon and that trend will often follow through till the next moon. Take this spell of wet weather right now, the last time we had more than a few dry days strung together was last month when the combines could go and many were making hay, so not a bad month. From the first of this month August, when it was the new moon the weather "broke" and we have rarely had two days dry stung together since. This trend in the weather will continue until the next new moon which is at the end of this month.

My prediction is that if the weather turns for the better in the first few days of next month, September, the chances are that it will stay in that trend for the whole of the next phase of the moon. Can you remember occasionally we get what they call an "Indian Summer" in September October time, well these weather periods last usually for the month or the phase of the moon. And if two of these weather patterns string along one after the other, we are usually in deep trouble, this is when the fields start going brown, or we get sodden ground with the seeds rotting in the fields and floods. So it all boils down to take what the weather throws at you and work with the weather, you can't change it. Trying to work against the weather is disastrous.

I recall the work mother used to put into her pantry to keep four of us lads growing and my dad and Uncle Jack as well. We had no Tesco's about then to feed the family most things came from the land we grew up on. A thing that everyone would like to go back to, but don't realize the work that this involved

I Remember Mothers Pantry

Mothers pantry six long shelves,
beams held bacon pair of hams,
At far end was safe for beef joint,
above a shelf for all the jams,
Kilner jars both empty and full,
filled top shelved four jars deep,
Bread in bin held six loaves,
lid on cheese and butter to keep.

She picked and peeled the fruit
she needed, all the summer long,
The pears she quartered packed
in tall jars, always with a song,
Sugar syrup was poured over,
till jar it over flowed,
The tops new seals were tightened lightly,
only till they're boiled.

Plumbs and damsons as they're
ready, they were done the same,
Birco boiler with false bottom,
all the jars to steam,
Six inches water turned on full,
fifteen jars it held,
One hour simmering lifted out,
lids firm on as if to weld.

When they cooled the lids were
tested, lose ones she re-boiled.
On the shelves she did put them,
with all the jars she'd toiled
Onions beetroot eggs and gherkins,
also cabbage red,
All the shelves were filled to
bustin, right up to the bin for bread.

Sunday morning father lifted,
down his twelve bore gun,
Down far field he was looking,
for a rabbit run,
Just disturb them in the long grass,
let them have a barrel,
Pick it up and gut it, dove tail
back legs, it won't quarrel

Hang it two days to let meat set,
mother skins it like a vest
Head and feet off for the pan,
quartered all the rest,
Short crust pastry then is rolled,
to fasten down the top
Blackbird pie vent then is fitted,
poured down its beak the stock.

Rabbit pie hot for dinner,
or its better cold,
With bread or taters it tastes good,
crust all big and bold,
It should be served along with
what, all rabbits love to eat,
Carrots cabbage turnips sprouts,
peas and lots of leeks

When it comes to chicken,
or its more likely an old hen,
Mothers really mustard ,
as she walks around the pen,
Looking for the one, that's
not broody or in lay
The poor old thing, ring its neck,
without undue delay.

When it comes to geese and
ducks, they're dealt the same,
Dressing them as we all watch,
the cat from outside in she came,
Neck chopped off she would
remove, wind pipe from the duck,
Then to her mouth she put and blew,
out came a startling quack.

On the geese removed the feet,
at knee joint half way up,
The sinews had to be pulled out,
or leg they would be tough,
On handing us the feet with long,
Sinews hanging out,
We pulled to make webbed stretch n close,
causing us to shout.

The butcher came to kill the pig,
upon the bench he put him,
Scalding water washed all over,
scrape hair up to his chin,
Lifted up to highest beam ,
his guts they did remove,
We kids learnt more of what to
store, of this we did approve.

Some pork was given out, to
whom killed pigs at different time,
Shoulder sides and hams were
salted, fat was rendered down,
Loved the scratching nice and crispy,
lard stored all in jars,
Hams and sides covered in muslin,
hung in pantry by my pa.

Pastry she did make on Sat dee,
we kids could help to taste
Mince pies jam tarts large n
small, we always had what's left,
Dried currants by the hand full,
spread on just half the doe,
Flapped over rolled and pressed,
in the oven would go.

It always gained some colour,
the pastry in our hands,
Hands got cleaner, with the rolling
cutting with the bands,
Out of oven,
each of ours did come,
Eaten as they hit the table,
never left a crumb.

A mouse trap fully loaded,
　　behind the pantry door,
With lump of stale cheese,
　　standing on the floor,
It was always at the ready,
　　in case invaders came,
They never stood a chance
　　get fat, always us to blame.

Mother tected pantry door,
　　but never it was locked,
We always knew what she had got,
　　neeth the jars she stacked,
So all my life the pantry loaded,
　　to the gunnels' high,
We lads we never felt pain of hunger,
　　like mouse that we deny.

———

**God gives every bird its food,
But he does not throw it into its nest.**
　J G Holland----

Chapter 4

A Bit Long in the Tooth

I know this is up to date but it will give you an insight into the bloke who's writing this book. I am trying to see myself as others may see me, in other words a reflection.

He's had seventy years in farming, getting a bit long in the tooth, although he's still got all his own teeth, moving a bit slower, standing a bit shorter, gone grey on top and can see his scalp through thin hair, got no work in him, looked after by his misses too well for his own good, and now got a new arm chair.

I Will Describe This Man I See

I will describe this man I see,
as best as I can judge,
When he sits down to have a rest,
job to make him budge,
This he does each afternoon,
till cup of tea at three,
Then slowly moves and back to work,
peel him off settee. (New chair now)

He used to have to duck his head,
go through six foot door,
Getting round shouldered,
natural bend, don't duck any more,
Gone all grey, going thin on top,
you see his scalp when wet,
Forehead getting higher,
no longer does he sweat.

When he gets a grump ,
lips turn down, jutting out his chin,
Eyebrows drop and looks through
them, run you must begin,
Its just a passing cloud I think,
the sun comes out and smiles,
Can just see his teeth, and the gap,
nothing them defiles.

Lazy comes to mind sometimes,
but then he's getting old,
Hasn't got his dad now,
to crack the whip and scold,
His own boss, do what he likes,
no one to whip him up,
All the ploughing matches been
to, he's only won one cup.

Another clue to who it is,
he had an operation on his knee,**
Then he had another just the same,
on the other you see,
Metal joints he had fitted,
these clues give you the key,
Must be why I'm shorter now,
for in the mirror, it's only me.

**I will tell you the story of my stay in hospital when I had both my knee joints replaced, but that will be for another day.*

In the meantime I was lucky enough to have a new arm chair for me birthdee. I was allowed to choose it and try it so there would be no moaning. Not that I ever moan, but I make exception about what they had to pay for it (moan), but then if I can have it for the next thirty years I suppose it will be okay. Oh now when I wake up in me chair, I find that the grand children have stuck the fridge magnets on my metal knee's. And they frighten themselves to death when they're trying out the new metal detector. It takes the best part of a minute (moan) to get out of it when it's in the extreme prone position, and when they bring a hot cup of tea, nobody wants to wait while I recover and sit up enough to be able to hold it, and when someone knocks the door (moan), they're just off out of the gate in the car by the time I get to them.

So the chair has some drawbacks, but by god it is comfortable.

This Comfortable Chair of Mine

Now I've turned seventy,
the family bought me a chair,
I had it for me birthdee,
I was consulted and aware,
Had to have a go try it out,
to make sure it did the job,
High enough back n' foot rest,
n' not too soft a squab.

Its huge when it stands there,
and a cable from the plug,
A controller in ya right hand,
and I fit in it nice and snug,
A button to lift ya feet up,
and a button to lower the back,
And one to lift you up again,
was soon getting into the knack.

Now I fear a power cut,
when me feet are up in the air,
Back is down and ya feel a clown,
conner git art o' the chair,
Like a tortoise on its back,
belly up swinging ya feet,
Shouting fa help come and get me,
help me git art o' this seat.

This hasn't happened but I fear,
could when I'm home alone,
Going to sleep that is easy,
but then I shouldn't moan,
If someone knocks at the door,
takes while to lift me right up,
They knock again and again,
I feel like a fly blown old tup.

I tell you the cover is leather,
cow hide has gone into that,
The cost of it was tremendous,
cow she must have been fat,
What we paid got short changed,
insides the cow had gone,
Price of the chair, price of cow,
beef and steaks we had none.

Now Ove got used to it,
inhabitations flew out of the door,
Sit in it after lunch and tea,
to sleep and have a good snore,
Appreciation what they bought,
suits me down to the ground,
Thank my family again and again,
this comfortable chair they found.

It is better to keep your mouth closed and let people think you are a fool than open it and remove all doubt
Mark twain (1835-1910)

Chapter 5

Village Craftsmen

Up until the 1950's almost every village had all the regular craftsmen that covered all aspects of village life, from the nurse come midwife, to the wheelwright who not only laid out the deceased made the coffin and dug the grave, and pulled the four wheel hand pulled hearse, then made or repaired farm carts, made ladders, wheelbarrows, gates, and everything in between.

A brick layer on the estate maintenance, a cobbler who mended and made boots and shoes and made and repaired horse harness, a shop keeper, a school, the vicar and of course the blacksmith, not forgetting the pub. There was nine farms that surrounded the village five of which were in the center, all the farms milked cows, and around 4pm in the afternoon herds of cows walking on the village roads in all directions, to their respective farms from outlying day pastures.

The Blacksmiths Shop around the 1950's

Mr. Giles travelled from Stafford to Seighford for two and sometimes three days a week; he also had a forge in East gate Street Stafford. With the number of horses rapidly declining it did not justify a full time blacksmith in the village. His main job was shoeing, welding repairing and fabricating gates and fences. Outside the blacksmiths shop was a heavy cast iron round disc, about 5ft across; to clamp wooden wheels down to while it was being hooped. To the extreme right, at the chimney end was a tall narrow furnace, the inside dimensions being only 18inches wide, but 6ft high and six foot long to heat up the wheel hoops to hammer them onto the wooden wheels. The original doors still cover the windows, but then they were just opening, no glass. This furnace had a crude steel door to make the draught draw under the gap at the bottom, and through the fire grate and up through the depth of coke, to provide the heat. The fumes joined the chimney that is still there to this day. This furnace had quite thick walls and an arch at the top, then a depth or sand on top to help keep the heat in a tiled roof to keep the weather out. To the left of the double doors was a large pile of sweepings out of the shoeing bay, comprising of hoof trimmings and filings, dried on mud carried in the horse's hooves, and whatever the horses cared to leave behind. Through the double doors was the shoeing bay where the horses were tied up. Then through a door immediately on the right, the first thing you saw in the middle was the anvil, this stood on a large piece of elm log to bring the top of the anvil to about two and a half foot high, handy hammering height. To the left was a pile of worn out horse shoes, some with nails still in.

On the right fastened to a bench was a metal bending tool to form the hoops for cart wheels, this could be adjusted to how tight the bend needed to be. The strip of flat iron would be heated then the end fed over the first roller under the second and over the third. A big cranking handle turned the rollers the middle roller was screwed down to put pressure to curve the metal. The next along the bench was a large blacksmiths vice this had a heavy bracket along the front edge of the bench, and a leg down into the floor. It had well-worn jaws that had gripped and been hammered for what seemed to be generations.

Also on this bench in front of the second window was a pillar drill, this had a large flywheel that turned horizontally above your head and a crank handle underneath was a huge chuck and a small vice to hold the metal while being drilled.

At the far end of the shop is the forge, this was made of bricks. At the front was an arch about eighteen inches high, by three feet wide with all sorts of scrap metal (useful off cut is the term I'm looking for) stuffed under for safe keeping. The top edge of the forge the bricks had a rounded edge then nine inches in it was filled up with fine coke. The hearth was open on two sides, and bricked round on the other two with metal lining to protect it from the heat .Over the top was a metal hood with inches of dust on it leading into a brick chimney.

At the back of the forge were the bellows, at one time, before I can remember he used the old bellows worked by foot pedal, made out of leather? These stayed there for quite a number of years, but got hidden by the "useful off cuts" but now the blowing was done by electric fan. All round the front and sides of the forge, except where he stood, were brackets holding all the tongs and tools of the trade. On the wall forming the left hand side of the hearth was his office; this took the form of a couple of nails with notes thrust onto them. One held the draughtsman's drawings of some fabrication job he had to do (drawn freehand on a torn off piece of cardboard full of thumb prints) one of many that had been put on before it. The other nail held an assortment of his wardrobe leather aprons jerkins and leggings that were in varying stages of dilapidation, the oldest at the back, right up to his older cap used when shoeing horses on the top. He had to reach just under this pile to operate the switch for the new electric fan.

First job when he arrived in a morning would be to light the forge, with a few sticks on crumpled newspaper. This was lit and the fan put on low, as the flames got enthusiastic some coke was gradually pulled over the burning sticks, and within a couple of minutes the fire was hot enough to boil the kettle. The fan was turned off and the fire would remain dormant most of the day.

Alongside the forge was a rusty dousing tank three quarters full of equally rusty water, where metal that needed cooling quickly was dunked in with a tremendous fizzling on the end of his tongs. At the back of his work shop was a rack that held new metal of all dimensions, some for horse shoes some for cart wheel hoops, some for making gate hinges and all the ironwork needed when the wheelwright was making a new cart or wagon plus everything in between. This had to be reached by climbing over, jobs waiting to be done, things taken in as patterns and all the useful off cuts that might come in handy

 The only clear floor area was from the door to the forge and round the forge, then round the anvil. Every so often they would fire up the furnace at the end of the blacksmith's shop for hooping wheels that Mr Clark the wheelwright had made or repaired. The hoops would be lifted out red hot and burned onto the wooden wheel that was clamped firmly on a huge cast iron disc that was permanently on the frontage of his shop. When hammered down into place firmly, water would be poured on to cool the iron hoop and shrink it tight onto the wooden wheel, these would then be rolled across the road and leaned against the wooden fence opposite, as many as twenty five of all sizes and weights ready to be repainted and refitted to their respective vehicles.

 On certain days of the week he would concentrate on shoeing horses mainly shires some cobs or float horses and a few hunters. When our two remaining shires wanted shoeing we would be lifted up on top of them and set off to school, Mr. Giles would lift us down to continue to school, then on the way home for dinner we would be pushed back on top to take them home again. Sometimes he would let us switch his forge fan on to heat a horse shoe, the shoe on the end of his tongs he would bury it in the center of the burning coke for about a minute, and it would come out more than red hot but going white hot with little sparks jumping off it.
This would hold the heat while he burned it onto the trimmed hoof of the shire, this made the shoe touch the

hoof all the way round and bed it in amid clouds of smoke. The shoe was then cooled before nailing it onto the horses hoof, the new set of shoes would last 6 to 8 weeks depending on the roadwork do. I can still hear the ringing of the anvil as the blacksmith pummeled the soft hot metal into the desired shape, after every blow to the metal he was working with there would be at least two smaller bounces of the hammer on the anvil creating a very sharp ringing, then two or three blows to the hot metal quite a dull sound. As the metal cooled to a dull red it would harden again and have to be reheated then the finer touches would be made turning it over and around until it reached the shape he wanted. It was a very hot job, sleeves rolled up and a heavy leather apron on, his cap turned slightly more than when he was cool and tipped back a little. Everything he used was shiny made so with the palm of his hardened hands that held the skill of many years of experience.

The blacksmiths shop closed around 1975 as did the wheelwrights, horses had reached their lowest numbers, with no shires at all in this district, but riding horses and ponies are on the steady increase and mobile farrier are taking over. The demand for wooden carts and wagons gradually came to an end as tractors with hydraulic tipping became more popular.

This was the blacksmiths shop in Seighford in 1945 when we were going to Seighford School. The tall narrow door on the right, was a furnace in which the iron hoops were heated red hot then hammered over the wooden wheel, which was clamped tight on the cast iron circle, permanently situated outside his shop.

I Remember Blacksmiths Shop

I remember blacksmiths shop,
all dingy dark and dusty,
Great big pile of horse shoes outside,
all a going rusty,
Tom Giles was smithies name,
all jolly strong and hot,
With shoeing father's horses,
he did the blooming lot.

When setting off to school one
morn, horses we would take,
To blacksmiths shop for shoeing,
would make us very late,
On going home for dinner,
these horses we would ride,
Pitched up high on Flower,
the others led with pride.

Welding cutting bending shaping,
everything was there,
To make it new, or fettle up,
to make a good repair,
His stock of metal had a rack,
but most of it had missed,
It lay in piles around his forge,
which was in its midst.

All day you'd hear the hammer,
a ringing out aloud,
Hitting out the red hot metal,
made him very proud,

The different shapes and sizes,
    needed for a gate,
Lay around the workshop floor,
    no need for him a mate.

Alone he worked all day until;
    we kids came out of school,
Then he would be invaded,
    his metal then would cool,
On his forge he put his kettle,
    there to make some tea,
We kids tried his drilling tool,
    great flywheel turned by me,

With tongs we tried to heat the
    metal, in the furnace hot,
To make and shape we would try,
    to bend on anvil, but,
Not hot enough to work it,
    so pumping the bellows up,
It made sparks fly everywhere,
    our school cloths covered us.

The water in the blacksmiths
    shop, warm to wash our hand,
With dowsing all the things he'd
    made, hot metal into bands,
With cloths soiled and singed,
    and not a hole in site,
Mother knew where we had been,
    said, late it's nearly night.

Education is not the filling of a pail, but the lighting of the fire. W B Yeats

Chapter 6

You May Like To See My Tractors

It seems that you young un's would be interested in what tractors I've got, well tonight we'll stick to the up to date ones, well I think they are, but they're an old man's choice, driven steady, cleaned now and then, oil changed on time and sometimes even greased.

First there is the Fastrac, at the moment I am hedge cutting, done most of mine, and now started on my contract customers.

Had a stone go through the lower door window last year and replaced it with a plastic green house panel, glued it in, you would never know if I hadn't said, and now the rear rounded glass quarter panel is badly cracked, so a bit late, I have fitted some wire mesh to protect it.

Next is the Deutz Agrotron it 85hp and today we had some yearling heifers eat their way through a briar patch and got into the wood, so I have got the post knocker on and been fencing. I fitted the brackets for the knocker to go on the front, it's a lot easier to see what your doing and you can reach on top of hedge banks, and across ditches, but having a longer hydraulic pipe slows the drop of the hammer a bit, but I can live with that.

This was Matt's tractor, and as it turned out, it pulled a farm trailer, his granddads three ton fergy trailer, with his coffin on, on his last journey to his grave. (See the story of Matthew in my earlier blogs). The tractor is just turning up ten thousand hours on the clock and looks like it could do the same again.

We have broken some windows and the frameless door, when mowing with a disc mower on seeds. Every pane of glass is curved and by gad they are expensive to replace, the insurance people (NFU) slapped a big surcharge, we pay the first fifty quid each time.

The Land Rover Discovery

It once belonged to a business man, who occasionally pulled a caravan, and had over a hundred thousand miles on the clock, I don't think it had ever seen mud, but now its seeing real life, pulls the stock trailer, and a three ton flat trailer, also the small trailer in the picture

    I took some scrap metal to the scrap yard eight miles away, the outfit was snaking and twisting if I went over thirty miles an hour, and over the weigh bridge I had got just short of four tons on board.

    Then on an uphill junction halt sign had to drop it into low range to be able to pull away, so I think it will have come to its last home. In the picture its got the small trailer hitched up, this saves having to chuck very dirt thing in the back

    Also in the picture you see that my loader on the Agrotron will not stack the bales more than three high in the barn, but then we have quite a long hay barn so we still have plenty of room. In the back ground is the three ton trailer loaded up with an old Fordson Elite three furrow plough and a matching furrow press. Sixty years ago that was the bees knees, they fitted a three row seed box on top of the press and you drilled the wheat as you ploughed and it had a following harrow to cover the seed. Job done all in one pass, probably about five or six acres a day. This outfit is pulled by my Fordson E27N but I'll show you that on another occasion.

This is another quote but I don't know who said it.
When the going gets too easy, you may be going downhill.

Chapter 7

My Operation to have new Knees

I kept an eye on the papers in case a surgeon from Stafford hospital had been relegated to Knackers man's assistant.—

In our late teens when as lads, like lads do, you act a bit macho, feel strong as an "ox" , and on looking back the men working on the farm took advantage and would egg us on to carry things three or four times what you are allowed to now a days.

When the threshing set came the grain had to be carried fifty or so yard, and up some brick steps into the loft to store ready for crushing through the plate mill to be fed to the cows. They would fill a large sack, wind it up on the sack hoist and get us lads to take it. They could have a good laugh as the younger of us struggled in wobbly strides platting our legs under the weight.

Wheat to go for milling was always required to be in one and half hundredweight sacks, (that's 75kilo in new money) and the seed wheat often came in two hundredweight sacks (100Kilo). All this carrying weights of that sort, brought about my knee problems starting in my fifties, which eventually I went to see what could be done to alleviate my painful arthritic knees.

You see the cartilage in the knee joint had worn out like a bush in a bearing, only it had worn out more on the inside of each joint making me very bow legged. Standing with my feet together there was almost six inches day light between my knees. When the old men were seen out and about walking bow legged father always used to say "their pig stopping days are over". Well mine had time had come now as well

This is the story of my operation to have new knees

Knees & Teeth

It was back in the 1990's that my knees started to feel as though they were wearing out, and as time went on I started to become bow legged. Also they became quite painful with arthritis, to the extent that I saw the doctor (I don't think he knew me by the dust he blew off my file).

He in turn referred me to a specialist, who parted me with a whole wallet full of cash, up at Rowley Hall private hospital. On entering the car park I found it essential that my old Montego car should be parked at the rural end of the car park underneath a laurel bush, at least only half the car could be seen and that way it might be the gardener's car, or some other menial leaning on a brush. On entry my feet seemed to disappear into a deep pile carpet, just as well knowing my ability at polishing shoes, I had new socks and pants just to impress the surgeon, as I guessed he might want my bags down.

After the seemingly compulsory half hour wait beyond the appointment time, my name was called, I don't know why as I was the only one present. After being ushered into an interview room, or perhaps it was a small lecture room. Mr. Travlos the consultant sat with a silent colleague some two feet higher than me in a very intimidating way. From where I sat you could see a polished seat to his trousers, and an unblemished sole to his shoe, as he sat very low with one leg crossed (his shoes had never trod in the crustations mine had and I have yet to take mine off).

After preliminary introductions the first question was "why do you think you need new knees "then he went through all the things why I should not have them done. This included gangrene and the loss of my leg or legs (I've no doubt through his incompetence) this gave me grave doubts about why I had bothered to unload so much money at the door. (Come to think about it I could have taken the Montego through the car wash about twenty times and enough change for a couple of tins of Kiwi polish for my shoes as well).

After ten minutes continuous confidence busting he decided to look at one of my knees , I don't know why when with my bags off he could see the other one as well, the other leg was on the chaise long not four inches away, perhaps that is what they call tunnel vision. Or perhaps I had only paid enough for one, you know how inflation takes hold when you're not up to date with things. One kneecap was excessively exercised and vigorously prodded, then it was left for me to decide if I would have a arthroscopy.

This I was told was to be done at the North Staffs (on NHS I must say), where an endoscope with a nipper would be sent under my kneecap to pullout debris, it must be the remains of my cartilage. This eventually was carried out only to find it had already disappeared, or most of it, so all that trouble for no benefit. Then I had regular appointment every six months for the next four years, each time the excuse was that I was not old enough. I was not too bothered about this although it was becoming very painful to live let alone walk, and in the back of my mind Mr. Travlos was getting valuable experience.
        (I kept an eye on the papers in case a surgeon from Stafford hospital had been relegated to a Knackers man's assistant)

At the beginning of 2001 the surgeon eventually gave me an appointment, this had a few preliminary appointments, with firstly the nurse to establish which one was to be done first. She told me to see my dentist, as bad teeth could poison my system and cause a rejection, with the worst scenario being loss of my leg.

Panicked by this I instantly found a dentist who promptly got me to sign a direct debit on the first day, and because of the urgency examined and counted my teeth on the second day, then on the third day scrapped and polished. This was my second in a lifetime brush with a dentist, the first time was in 1946 at Seighford School at the age of eight, when a dentist set up his chair in the main hall and all the kids were examined in turn. He found nothing then and they found nothing now, but six months down the line, at the next appointment it was different. With a sharp hook he counted my teeth and when he thought there was nothing to do he dug his hook deep into the top of a tooth and declared it needed filling. Another appointment for the filling that was not needed, and another again for the scrape and polish. Then apart from my monthly standing order he extracted another sixty quid. Never in my life have I ever felt so ripped off by a professional who put no more than three minutes to drill and fill the tooth that he had violated.

They are still drawing my money every month, and now I've missed three six monthly appointments. I do still go to the dentist more regular now, every six months to get my money's worth, but all the dentist does is count them, not else, then a scrape and polish. I am told at home I should be ashamed of myself as I have never brushed my teeth in my life, but I am the only one with all good teeth, and that makes the family cross.

After all the preliminary checks and rechecks my appointment came through, On the two weeks run up to this date we had a vigorous reappraisal of my clothing, shorts seemed to be high on the list as after care involved constant attention and exercise

The anesthetist came to examine me and gave reassuring utterances, then Mr. Tavloss with his minion's one of whom produced a felt tip pen at his demand, and slapped into his palm as if it were a knife. This is what we are faced with, do what you can, was the reading I took from their faces, as they marked out my knee with arrows.

By this time I had almost got to know what a true gentleman Mr. Travlos was and had every confidence in his abilities. On one preliminary appointment I overheard him negotiating with a supplier over the quality of his replacement joints claiming they had a longer wear life than those previously supplied, perhaps from Taiwan.

The morning of the Knife came, NILL BY MOUTH was hung round my neck, (or should I say on my cupboard), by mid-morning my belly thought my throat had been cut. But in the mean time I was handed a bottle of what looked like iodine, a gown and an empty tea bag, called pants (to pull on to hold my body and soul together) , and then to the shower. Emerging from the shower looking like I had got a very deep sun tan after pulling on my "tea bag", (in your hand it was no bigger than an small envelope with three holes) and a back to front gown that I could not tie. A hard board had been placed under my new sheet on the bed, and the bed made like an "apple pie" bed, while I was in the shower, this I found out a little later was so they could slide me across easily onto the trolley that took me to theatre.

The waiting room of the theatre had beautiful pictures on the walls, and to cater for those like myself who were prone, and nervous, and a fixed gaze skywards , there was pictures on the ceiling as well. My appointed time was up and the trolley was shoved into a small room with the walls lined with, bottles tubes syringes and all the thing to put you under, (and I presume to bring you round as well)

The anesthetist, who had given me an examination the day before, was along side of me reaching for his utensils, and on turning round, a large needle pointing upward was dripping, (the time had come). In my mind when the theatre doors opened was the image of three persons with yard brooms throwing down buckets of water, to make the operating room clean again for me to go in, (slaughter house stile). But in fact in came a man or woman dressed in mask and gown and gloves, and until he spoke did not realize it was Mr. Travlos himself.

How privileged I felt, to be welcomed by the head (or knees) man himself. Then thirty second later, the dripping needle was plugged onto a tap already put in a vein on the back of my hand. The clock above the theatre door was the last thing I saw, saying ten thirty five and twenty seconds. Then out like a light. The next thing I knew was looking through a fog at the ceiling of the recovery room, some two hours later I believe. And when fully conscious I was wheeled back to the ward.

That evening all my visitors were keen to see my bandages, (and so was I) there must have been four inches of wading and bandage from well up my almost to my ankle, with three drainage pipes out of the top, leading into vacumeised bottles under the bed. The knee was soar but the continuous pain of arthritis, had noticeably gone.

The next morning I enjoyed my breakfast, and could have eaten it four times over, but more pressing matters were building up, notably toilet variety. Passing water was no problem, in fact it took a while to get used to pee'ing up hill, into a bed bottle. Then twenty four hours on that privilege was quietly withdrawn to encourage you walk to the toilet. It was now time to get my feet onto the "deck" to start walking.

The nurses were busy getting others moving, so I thought I would get my feet out on my own. The heavy leg was gradually wriggled towards the side of the bed, poking across with my free foot. This was very painful, but then again that was nothing compared to what was about to happen. After ten minutes of maneuvering and bracing myself for the big drop, one quick nudge of my free foot sent the bandaged leg lowering rapidly to the floor and nearly sent me through the roof. Of course it would not bend, and the jar of arriving suddenly to the floor reverberated back up to my knee. On biting my lip so hard it was what to do next. Eventually I was assisted back up onto the bed, but only to pull out the drainage pipes, these I felt ran down under the stitches to varying lengths, they gave me something to bite so it took no working out what was to come.

Sure enough pain was something to get used to in here, and out came the pipes, and the bandages were changed and reduced. For the first time the plaster was revealed that was stuck on the stitches, this was clogged with dried blood and had set hard. At this stage I found out that it was blood from the slaughter houses, that they stuck plywood together with not so many years ago. However my plaster resembled plywood.

Next on the scene was the physiotherapist, to begin the torturous process of bending the knee to forty five degrees before I can go home, a process that took about three or four more days. Fist and the most urgent was to be able to get to the loo, as the bottles had been cleverly withdrawn. This was achieved with a walking frame, and being advised on how to use it by the phisio. That afternoon the urge to pass water came about me and under normal circumstances I would have ten minutes to think about it and ten more to get there.

But things had changed, slowly out of bed with my feet and on with the slippers, (you never know what you might find on the loo floor in bare feet) Up onto the frame and shuffle along to the loo, a short wait before it became available, the other loo was at the other end of the ward, and the pressure was such that that was ruled out. In to the loo and up to the pan, up one leg of the shorts and the relief and pleasure it was to let the water flow , only to find the lining of the sports shorts was a net through which I was reliving myself. Never in my life have I ever sieved the water I passed (pissed) down the loo.

The walking frame only lasted a day and we went onto elbow crutches, and the early warning signs of wanting the loo were heeded immediately, that gave much needed walking practice The day before I came out they took me to the stairs to practice going up and down with the elbow crutches - lead with the good leg going up, lead with the bad leg going down. A couple of visits from Mr. Travlos and his team and another on his own to confirm my release, reveled the man behind the knife, to be a very caring perfectionist, who had plenty of people to practice on in the few years before my turn came.

He had time to sit and talk for a while, generous with his time as well his skills. My appreciation of this man knows no bounds,] and have recommended him to all who will listen. The second knee was operated on by the same man six months later, having had the earlier experiences, it went smoothly in the knowledge of what I learned then. It should be my next intention to get to know my dentist in the same way, but without any pain I think this to be most unlikely.

Now just a few private thoughts on teeth

Teeth are nature's way

Teeth are nature's way,
of grinding to recycle,
They provide one with,
expression that is vital,
That sparkling star that,
emerges from your lips,
Through them passes everything,
that goes onto the hips.

Some peoples teeth they rot away,
but still they put on kilo,
Even when their chin comes up,
no teeth to fill the hollow,
Wonder how the mirror stands
it, each and every day,
Fitting false teeth mashers,
or gum food to a puree.

The dentist loves to see them
coming, sitting in his chair,
Please make me a new set,
the old ones beyond repair
False teeth got wiped off
drainer, along with tater peelings,
Thrown up the back of ess hole*,
along with all the fillings.

Ess hole, bottom of the chimney in an old cast iron kitchen range)

New dentures rub ya gums sore,
or drop out in your dinner,
Can't eat as quickly as before,
help you get much thinner,

Daren't cough or sneeze or even
fart, look after this new set,
Cost a fortune them to make,
no more chewing on briquette

Nuts at Christmas they are
out, so is tough old beef,
Only things that you can squash,
tween those brand new teeth,
They spend more time in jar,
up in the bathroom cupboard,
Than where they should be,
more lip there to be puckered.

So the lesson here I see, look
after the teeth your born with,
No need for dentist's help at all,
and sweep away the myth,
Teeth should last a lifetime,
still there when y're only bones,
Looking upwards in repose,
smiling up beneath gravestones.

If you're going to kick authority in the teeth, you might as well use two feet.
Quotation by **Keith Richards**

Chapter 8

Two More of my Tractors

But me I stick with the old stuff that I was brought up on and the ploughs and implements that matched them.

Now into September were into the ploughing match season, entry forms all filled in and time to get the old ploughs and tractors ready for a bit of steady work. Round our local matches they have classes for young farmers on the modern outfits, big reversible ploughs, and they always bring their biggest and best. But me I stick with the old stuff that I was brought up on, I have tried in my way to replicate the old tractors the father had new, he of coarse had his Standard Fordson, I have not acquired one of those yet, but I did acquire a Fordson E27N, which is the long legged version of the Standard (the blue one here) Fordson, same 27hp engine and three gears and a reverse.

It's not till you get on one of these old machines that you realize how far tractors have developed.

When fathers E27N came about 1950 it was very up to date at that time with three point linkage and a power take off and it had side brakes to help with the turning on wet ground, all of which the Standard did not have.

Then when I was in my late teens we had a David Brown Cropmaster, this was TVO and you still started it with a crank handle.

Following that we had the International B250, *(see on the previous page part restored and fully restored)* this was a diesel and it had a diff lock, this is the tractor that I drove from new and have been responsible for ever since. Basically it got retired years ago and put in the tin shed, tin shed rotted away and the rain got down the exhaust pipe.

I drove this tractor from new in 1956; it stood unused for almost twenty five years and now it is over fifty years old, it's been brought back to life. Here it's had the engine done the wheels and back end have been painted, the bonnet engine and gear box have yet to be cleaned up, but that was back in 2005.It is now fully painted up in its original livery and almost looks like new, we have taken both these tractor on road runs, but this one's max speed is twelve miles per hour, the E27N will do a bit faster if pushed

My old Tractor-International B250

My old tractor standing there,
for years its not been started,
Drove it myself from new,
and now almost departed,
Roof is blown off the shed,
and it's rained in down its pipe,
The engines well stuck and
rusted, on the inside full of gripe.

For fifty years I've have had it,
while working never faltered,
Apart from rust and lack of paint,
appearance never altered,
Got to save it now before,
it rots and rusts away,
To pull it out and look at
it, do it straightaway.

Some tyres flat and perished,
they will still hold some wind,
Enough to carry it to shed,
where it can be re-tinned,
Off with bonnet wings and wheels
can see it undressed now,
Get into heart of engine see,
if can put it back to plough.

Water in two cylinder,
have rusted pistons solid,
Sump comes off to loosen;
big ends then are parted,
Hammering and thumping,
to get the pistons out,
New set of liners n pistons now,
cheque book time to clout.

Got new shells for big ends,
and set of gaskets too,
Back together now and see,
what there is next to do,
Injector pump with lid off,
is pushing up stuck springs,
With little bit of persuasion,
knock down plunger fittings.

New injectors they are fitted,
valves are well ground in,
On with lively battery,
to turn it mid smoke and din,
Firing up it comes to life,
from near scrap recovered,
Can concentrate efforts now,
look better newly colored

Bought new wings n new nose
cone, olduns full of dents,
Standing on its jack stands,
it's far from those events,
Gunk and solvents' liberally,
to wash the oil and dirt,
Lying on your back beneath,
it all gets on your shirt.

Ready for the primer now,
and get in all the corners,
Always find some bits not
clean, drips along the boarders,
Rub it down where paint has run,
ready for its top coat,
Don't want dust or flies or damp,
gloss I must promote.

Front n back wheels now back on,
brand new shiny nuts,
New exhaust enamel black,
tin pan seat to rest your butt,
Fit the loom n lights n switches,
oil gauge and ammeter,
Needs new steering wheel and nut,
to set it off the neater.

Out on road run we have booked,
got a logbook too,
On red diesel it runs at home,
some run on white a few,
Insurance and a tax disc now,
new number plates as well,
Will miss my cosy heated cab,
frozen Christmas tail to tell.

Old tractors Large Old Tractors Small.

Old tractors large,
old tractors small,
Some go well,
some they stall,

Most are older,
than their owners,
Some run sweetly,
some are groaners.

Worn out tyres,
cracked and perished,
Rims all pitted with
rust and blemished,
Some come with
nose stove in,
Cut it off and chuck it in bin.

New bonnet it will
cost the earth,
Sprayed and polished,
look like new birth,
New chrome nut
for steering wheel,
To finish the tractor,
will give you zeal.

Wheel nuts painted or
new ones shiney,
New pins and clips,
on little chains o'h blimey,
These little touches
make the difference,
Get it noticed from a distance.

First thing you're told
when first you're out,
"That's not right shade",
and gives you doubt,
A clever clogs with
brush painted bonnet,
That's my old tractor,
he's to covet.

Quite a bit of competition,
Who's got the silliest seat cushion?
Hessian bag on tin pan seat,
Very original, but not so neat.

Every one becomes an expert,
Their influence on you exert,
Keep it original they say,
Fiber glass copies keep at bay.

A nice sweet engine,
like to hear,
New plugs and leads,
and wheel to steer
Throaty roar
when it's struck up,
Draw the crowds,
when you wind it up.

I Booked into a Ploughing Match

I booked into a ploughing match,
there to show my skill,
See how straight and even,
my opening split instill,
A moment's loss of concentration
blows the ideal apart,
Spend the rest of all that day,
looking like upstart.

Good many tractors on the field,
all likeminded to plough,
Markers out all over the place,
beyond the plots allow,

Down and back complete the split;
wait for judge to mark,
Close it up, flat top or pointed,
critical watchers remark.

Some pause for lunch walk to see,
how the neighbours done,
Body language tells it all,
a grimace purse of lips so glum,
They try to break your
confidence, concentration goes,
Look back see plough blocked up,
new expletives compose.

All best mates when ya make a mess,
condolences come in,
Very polite clapping best in class,
everyone wishing to win,
A jolly good bunch of ploughmen,
relax till judge is back,
See who's is best of the bunch,
and who has got the plaque.

This picture (above) was taken at home, we are not allowed to use the furrow press at ploughing matches, but it shows what a good job this sixty year old outfit can still do. It was intended for a three row seed drill used to be mounted on the press and a harrow dragged behind to cover the seed.

The Elusive Cup

A disappointing outcome to the Stafford ploughing match 16 September 2006 using the E27N and Elite plough for the first time. With no diff lock the land wheel was slipping leaving a loose stubble that blocked the plough on its next run up a slight slope. at the next two matches the following week I fitted the spade lug wheels and eliminated the slipping

The Elusive Cup

Off to the ploughing match
   with great intent
Good weather helps
   but the land is wet
Off down the field
   on the first run
Back up the second
   the twists begun.

Tipping in the third
   as though no skims
Blocking up the plough
   and the trouble begins
Coming up the fourth
   won't bury the stubble
Land wheel slipping
   and we're in trouble.

Off up the side of the
   neighboring plot
Tape measure out to see
   what we've got
To start the cast
   it must be parallel
Or the finish, odd sized
   will give you hell.

Even furrows with
   good in's and outs
Firm for a seed bed
   well turned over each bout
No hand work or gardening
   is ever allowed
But it happens quite
often when the judge turns around

To measure the land
each bout is a must
As narrow it gets down
to three or bust
The penultimate run
is always shallow
It's to hold the plough
firm as it turns its last furrow

Everyone's an expert
who watches your last run
But get in the seat to feel
how it's done
They block your eye line
at the end of the stint
All standing astride,
its all wavering and bent

Everyone says we must
not blame the tools
Not everyone there,
that we can call fools
Experience shows by
the polished plough
Who puts it away with
a tinge of rust now

Never again, and the
thought that it's rotten
When the next one comes
along and you've forgotten
Try once more for that
elusive red card and cup
The knees will go weak,
when you're eventually called up.

Me knees went weak with excitement only on two or three occasions. I'm not as good as some who seem to win every time, but it is the best man (or girl) who wins. Can't blame the tools, and if the plough went rusty over winter who forgot to oil the mole boards.

A man should not leave this earth with unfinished business, He should live each day as if it was a pre-flight check. He should ask each morning, am I prepared for lift-off?
    Diane Frolov and Andrew Schneider

Chapter 9

Father grew Sugar Beet

The tractor we used at that time was the David Brown Cropmaster, its wheels adjusted to the row crop widths for the beet and the Fordson Major was used to haul the crop to the station. It was after the war in the early 1950's that the new crop to our area was encouraged, Sugar Beet. Father had a contract, the factory supplied the seed, and the beet had got to be taken half a mile down the road to the sidings of Great Bridgeford station.

This is not Bridgeford Station but this was the same LMS (London Midland Scotland) loco as used to shunt trucks in and out of the sidings, these were the type of wagons in the picture.

The beet was loaded onto a 20 ton railway goods wagon with five days to get it loaded We had no elevator or anything in them days the beet had got to be thrown up into the truck the first half of the load could be thrown through the open door of the truck, but after that it was eight foot up even when standing on our beet trailer. The sugar beet pulp was sent by the beet factory by rail in a covered van type truck to the same siding. Of this you could only have your allocation according to what amount of sugar beet you sent in. These railway trucks were in the sidings at the station for only about five days, and then the shunter engine came and took them. The same applied to the coal trucks, the coal merchant had got to get it empty in that time.

At weekends we would go down to the station with the load of beet and sometimes we could go into the signal box with the signal man and warm up in front of his big potbellied stove. In the corner of the signal box was cardboard box with explosive detonators, these were clipped on the track when there was thick fog and train drivers could not see signals, bit close to the stove we thought. When the shunting engine came to collect trucks out of the sidings we were allowed to pull some of his levers, we were given a detonator to clip on the line for the shunted wagons to run over, it made an almighty bang.

Father Grew Sugar Beet

Father grew sugar beet,
for this he had a contract,
Corporation supplied the seed,
gave advice and backed,
Seed was sown on the flat,
didn't have to ridge,
Singling and weeding,
big gang with hoe's for tillage.

These look a bit like sweeds to me?

Had a side hoe on the tractor,
four rows at a time,
Just the weeds between the
plants, in May at their prime.
Once the beet leaves touched in
row, smothered all the weed,
Not much now to do, let them
grow the bulk what we need.

Lifting beet we had a tool,
firked under the roots of the crop,
Again its on the tractor,
to make it easier to pull and top,
Two rows pulled by leading man,
and laid across the rows,
Next 2 rows on top to wilt,
sugar from tops to root allows.

Beet is topped by hand into,
alternate piles of tops and beet,
Roots loaded onto biggest trailer,
taken to station did repeat,
Fill the wagon in the siding,
it takes twenty tons,
Got five days to load n fill,
then shunter collects full wagons.

Beet tops are fed to the cows,
right up to the turn of the year,
Loaded by hand and chucked on
grass, afore the cows appear,
They gave good milk and enjoyed,
and improved the yield,
Sugar Beet was a winner all round,
dam cold job across the field.

No precision drills and no rubbed and graded seed, so once the beet seedling came through they came in clumps and had got to be singled and gapped by hand with hand hoe's. The tractor steerage hoe cleared the weeds down the row which did four rows at a time, the man on the back steered the implement to follow the rows of seedlings closely.

I Remember Singling Sugar Beet

I remember singling sugar beet,
on Barn Field it was long,
Ten of us following close,
and talking in a throng,

Owd Tommy he was slow,
and he got left behind,
Ground was dry and dusty,
not enough to blind.

Now George he's in his thirties,
his bladder wouldn't hold,
Got to have a pee now,
halfway down the row behold,

He pee'd on top of Tommy's
row, and then he carried on,
Till Tommy came across a damp
spot, in his row dead on.

Further down we all watched,
as he stuck his finger in,
To see what had wet the earth,
held muddy finger by his chin,

> We all rolled with laughter,
> till told him what was on his paws,
> Poor owd Tummy takes a joke,
> short straw he always draws.

This is about an old man Tommy

    He lived and worked about the village all his life, he lived with his sister, and farmed a few acres made hay for his three cows and their calves. He had a big garden where he grew mangols for the cows, along with all the normal garden household produce. Tommy was in his sixties when we were growing up, and always came to help with singling the beet, though he was a bit slow, and helped to build the stacks and bays of wheat and oats.

    Then again when the thresher man came to the village, he followed that round all the farms. For the younger readers it took nine men to operate the old threshing box before the days of the combine. Tommy was often the butt of tricks, one of which was when he and Nelly had their first television, and had a new aerial put up on his chimney.

    We would be in our teens, and Tommy was "crowing" about what they had bought and about the expense. We also knew that he kept his now disused bowler hat on a peg just inside of his back door. So one dark night before he had locked his door we got hold of his bowler, brought up a long ladder from the farm, and with the aid if Nelly's washing line prop, and hooked his bowler on top of his new TV aerial. Well he could not get it down and there it stayed for quite a few weeks until a strong wind dislodged it.

    I know this is a long poem about him but you will

get a fair idea of the kind of man he was and how cheerful he was every day. He would be born in about 1890 (it's on his grave stone), so very old fashioned and traditional, hence his carpet bag

Owd Tommy Abbotts

Owed Tom Abbotts lived in a
cottage, with his sister Nell,
They kept three cows and calves,
and a few old hens as well,
Cattle grazed across four acres,
the rest was mown for hay,
In his garden he grew his mangols,
fed in short winters day.

He helped his neighbours,
when they're shorthanded,
With drilling hoeing weeding,
with others he was banded,
At harvest time he stacked bays,
till in the roof was bound,
Longest ladder then was cast,
him get back to ground.

All the years I knew him,
he always had some wit,
Smoked a pipe, chewed tobacco,
and showed us how to spit,
He had a bike sit-up-and beg,
handle bars reached his chest,
On Friday went to town on it,
his hat he wore his best.

His shopping bag hung on his
bike, a long carpet bag it was,
All stitched up on either side,
flat by front wheel because,

When was loaded it was safe,
hung by strong loops of cord,
If it was carried in his hand,
almost dragged with the hoard.

As a young man stood up
straight, he'd be five foot eight,
Old and stooped, round of back,
shorter still as life dictate,
Feet a splayed for easy stance,
and knees a slight of bend,
One thumb hooked in waist coat
pocket, tuther to pipe distend.

He always had a cheery smile,
his eyes were almost closed,
When he had dam good laugh,
tears ran down pointed nose,
His face was brown and ruddy,
from working in all weathers,
On his nose and chin could see,
red veins mapped his features.

On his feet were black boots,
well up above his ankle laced,
His trousers had a gusset, hold
his expanding tummy braced,
It was a different colour , and
could see when he bent over,
And buttons of his bracers ,
straining hard to cotton anchor.

Waistcoat matched his trousers,
a suit some point decide,
Ten buttons some were missing,
four pockets two each side,

One it held pocket watch,
secured to button hole with chain,
Another held his match box,
England's Glory was it by name.

His jacket didn't quite match,
been stitched around the collar,
Pockets drooped like open mouth,
weighed down as if to cower,
In one was his bacca pouch,
top pocket reserved for pipe,
Pipe was mostly in his mouth,
not always did he light.

He carried a little pocket knife,
his baccy Twist to cut,
When he rubbed it in his palm,
into his pipe he put,
With cupped hand around his
pipe, he lit it with a match,
Puff and suck till it was lit,
mid curls of smoke detach.

Eventually it went out again,
and back into top pocket,
Out with the Twist and cut a knob,
chew into old tooth socket,
This is where he learned all us
kids, to squit with baccy juice,
It went with long streak so far,
to reach his poor old goose.

Tommy had a bowler hat ,
kept on peg inside back door,
As kids he let us try it on,
and asked him what it was for,

It was used to go to town in,
now for only funerals touted,
He kept it brushed and steamed,
though it become out dated.

Now it was only flat caps,
that he was nare without,
Into town he used his best,
to walk around see whose about,
One was used, milk his cows,
grease and cow muck plastered
Nuther used round house and
village, not so much it mattered.

Tommy's ears were large and thin,
for a man so short,
Ragged round the top edge,
frost bite they must have caught,
They tucked back nice and even,
his cap they're there to hold,
His head he kept it nice and
warm, ears out in the cold.

His garden always nicely dug,
and cow muck spread a plenty,
Grew his household veg and
spuds, and runner beans a bounty,
The biggest plot was that of
mangols, for his pampered cows,
The three of them, bedded up,
roots chopped them to brows.

We called round my dad and me,
Nelly made us a cup of tea,
One of Tom's cows had calved,
others had dried off you see,

Milk she poured rich and yellow,
beastings from his old cow,
She had to stir most vigorously,
tea too rich to drink right now.

In winter time when he was younger,
Tom he carted coal,
Picked it up from Bridgeford
Station, Seighford was his goal,
(distance just over a mile)
Brought it over Bridgeford bank,
with donkey and a cart,
This it filled the time o'er winter,
before drilling corn did start.

So it was that he got too old,
to work about the farms,
Even gave up his cows and garden,
that he loved and charmed,
Then he lost his sister Nell,
and lived a few more years alone,
He himself succumbed to life,
both in Seighford neath headstone.

Quotation by Caesar Augustus (63BC-14AD
Young men, hear an old man to whom old men harkened when he was young

Chapter 10

The Long Harvest (1938—2008)

How the harvesting has change over the last seventy years, with the advent of bigger and better combines, you would wonder how it all got done years ago, but then it was sheer numbers of men and man power that was important then.

The earliest memories I have of threshing and the sale of wheat, which was about £18.00 a ton (1940's) was when the steamer came maneuvering into the stack yard with his threshing box baler and a trusser. The trusser tied the straw into batons, so the straw could be used to thatch next year's ricks or stacks. A few years on and they drove the thresher with a Field Marshal single cylinder diesel tractor. It was done this way up until mid-1950's when the first combine began to appear all of which were of the bagging variety. Still a lot of work collecting the sacks that had been dumped on the field, and it needed someone on the combine who tie the bags tightly as some burst open on impact sliding from the bagging platform high on top of the machine.

I Remember the Threshing Machine,

During the winter short of straw,
call in the threshing machine,
Ricks of corn all stacked and
thatched, oats peas and beans,
Mixed corn to feed the cows,
and straw to bed them up,
Ozzy Alcock on his steamer,
he brings his whole setup.

See the steam and smoke a
puffin, o'er bank before he's seen,
Calls at the pool by Seighford
Hall, for water he is keen,
Polish up with oily rag,
and oil can in his other hand,
Keep busy while the tank fills
up, next farm he's in demand.

His teeth have grip on his pipe,
swinging steamer into gate,
Some of the train leaves on
road, peg pulled out by his mate,
One at a time Box, Baler n binder,
positioned to get belt in line,
Steam engine last to shuffle in
place, start in the morning, nine.

Ozzy and his mate are here by
six, they travel about on bikes,
Light fire in the old steamer,
match from his pocket he strikes,
Oil all the dozens of bearings,
check the belts are all tight,
Time for breakfast and a brew
of tea, fill up his pipe to light.

Quarter to nine he opens regulator,
steam to the piston apply,
All the spindles and shafts and
pullies and belts all begin to fly,
Lot of dust rises from threshing
box, and sets to a steady hum,
Men from neighbouring farms
who help, know its time come.

It takes a whole day to thresh a
bay, just a bit more for a rick,
Onto the next farm up the village,
makes his way quite quick,
This is repeated around the farms,
about three times each year,
Dirty dusty job it was, not
looking forward for him reappear.

The Old Combine 1988-1997

It was always frustrating at corn harvest, to see the corn dry and ripe through a fine spell of weather, and then when the contractor eventually arrives, the weather breaks. My neighbour Reg at Green Farm had what then was a huge old combine, with a sixteen foot cut. He could pull into a twelve acre field at two pm. when the sun had got to its height, and by five it was completed. With a contractor, he starts when the due is off at ten am. At this time the grain could be too moist for storage and certainly too wet to sell, then expects to keep going until after dark. The opportunity came when Reg retired in the late 1980's, all his farm chattels were up for auction including the old Laverda combine.

This combine had started life in 1974 on a farm at

Milford, and also was one of the first of its make to appear in this country from Italy. It was the first one sold by Burgess'es, and the sales man said of it that it was built like a tank, and every model after that was built down from that (in other words a bit lighter metal here and less bolts there to cheapen its manufacture). When the farm at Milford sold up Reg bought it and it came to Seighford, it was kept under a tin shelter at the end of the hay barn. Every summer you would hear the distinctive roar of its engine burst into life, as it reversed out to begin yet another harvest. There were not many six cylinder engines about then particularly in our village, and this one ran as sweet as a nut.

It was the first time I had ever driven a combine, and its previous owner Reg came to get us started when the first winter barley was ripe. As with most old vehicles the alarm systems that warn you of impending blockages or slip clutches slipping did not work. The mice or the gremlins had pulled the wires off their connections, so the messages did not get through to the driving platform. (No such luxury as a cab on this one). In the weed seed box was such a device, weed seeds built up until the bag and the box was full, the pressure built up, the cross auger was compressing so tight that it was emerging like cow cubes, or expeller flakes. It had happened before, the flight of the auger were by now tapered like a cork screw, and had been very hot at different times. When tight enough the auger stopped and a slip clutch warning should blow the horn (A flap in the box was meant to warn of it being full before it got to this stage, but no wires.) The grain elevators stopped and there started a buildup on the shakers, then no straw movement within the combine. All this time the one hundred and twenty horses power, were turning the header and the drum, and almost every belt on the combine was slipping and smoking.

Sitting at the front amid the dust and noise with the wind in your face, it was only when you turned at the end and discovered that there was something burning or you wander where all the last swath of straw is. Then with a horrible thump the straw was regurgitated back into the drum, which stalled it big engine locking the drum solid, this left a massive blockage was then to be cleared, as the smoking belts had plenty of time to cool. The body was full of straw the sieves were blocked with grain, the grain elevators were chock full as well, all this from one small oversight of not emptying the weed seed box. That type of blockage was never repeated, as the weed seed box was then always left open for the weeds to return to the field, as it does on most other combines. It took two whole days to clear out and get running again then the third day was wet, but that's how it goes in farming, if everything ran perfect how boring life would be.

Another similar blockage occurred from a small cross auger in the grain box, this is driven by a small bike chain in a chain case, in turn driven by the elevating auger from the bottom of the combine. When the chain came off that too had a chain reaction, but by then you get to know when all is not well, and stop by instinct and minimized the extent of the blockage. It boiled down to a very expensive bevel gear box about the size of a big Mug putting the sprocket out of line for the chain. To overcome this chain and the bevel gear were pitched into the scrap ruck. A hole was ground with the angle grinder, through the side or the delivering auger, and a flap of metal welded at the top of its flights to push the grain into the grain box direct. We then found it important to keep the lid on the grain box as it sprayed the grain with much speed and efficiency, a modification that the manufacturers had not thought of.

When filling with fuel, it is not easy to get all of it into the fuel tank, and with the help of a gust of wind, some invariably misses. As the air intake is within eighteen inches of the fuel filler cap this sometimes gets a spray of fuel. With all air intakes, the larger particles of dust are screened on the outside with a wire gauze, and when this gets damaged an old sack doubles as a useful screen tied on with the inevitable piece of string. Now when the sack screen gets a soaking of diesel fuel, however inadvertently there will be trouble. (Although not apparent at the time) As the work day wares on, by midafternoon, when there is maximum dust and maximum heat, the dust builds up on the sack, and with being wet with diesel the dust turned to paste and starts to seal the air intake. A large powerful engine cannot stand being starved of air for long, the revs take a sudden dip, and a column of very thick black smoke emits from the exhaust. This is caused by the suction on the air intake, with no air, and starts to pull oil from the sump up past the pistons and then burnt and emitted as very dense smoke. There was enough smoke to stop the M6 motorway if the wind was going that direction.

Before I realized what the cause was, it rectified itself when the engine revs were reduced, then tried a few minutes later and the same happened again. On closer inspection it became very apparent, that the air intake was sealed and smothering it. A clean dry sack was all that it took to alleviate a very worrying half hour.

During the 1990's it became illegal to burn straw on the field, it had a very distinctive smell when burning, and the odor carried for miles down wind. So it was with great interest when reaching the highest point on the Cumbers field, to see where this illegal smell of smoke was coming. From that vantage point you could see nearly all the parish, and certainly see the origins of an illegal fire. The slow but deliberate three point turn that you do at the end of every bout, was a bit slower than usual for extra observation time, and no smoke was detected on any horizons.

Then it suddenly became clear that the burning straw (or in this case smoldering straw) was under the engine cover of my old combine. The dust and bits of straw had built up and fell onto the exhaust manifold, here it was being vigorously fanned by its own radiator cooling fan running full belt. On top of the combine we always carried a five gallon drum of water for just such an emergency, and with only seconds to spare live embers were being blown out of the engine compartment. The emergency was soon over within minutes, and damped down, and the offending dust cleared from the different ledges. The combining continued as if nothing had happened, but pleased that the water was to hand.

The gear box is essential, and when all the teeth of first gear get ground off, with all the carless gridding when going from reverse to forward, and second gear too fast for heavy crops, then something has to be done. Fortunately a second hand gearbox was sitting in Burgess yard and two days later it was going again.

In the years I had her, ten I think, bits would wear out and if they were not essential they would be decommissioned (thrown onto the scrap heap). This can only go on for so long, and a law of diminishing returns come into play. If an essential part has to be replaced to carry on, and when this part is more expensive than the whole combine is worth, then it's near the end.

On the last outing by the Ashes wood it caught fire, it was internal and the water we carried could not reach the seat of the fire. By the time the fire brigade came it was too late, and when they had gone it was sad to see the old hulk, blackened, the paint and the tyres burnt off, listing and dripping from the belated soaking it had just had. It lay where it had burned for almost two years before the scrap men could get to it, it was either too wet on the ground or the crops were in the way, and all ploughed ground to cross four field from the road.

The remainder of that year's crop was combined by contractor.

Quotation ------ **Knowledge is like a garden, if it is not cultivated, it cannot be harvested** (African Proverb)

Chapter 11

**Father Always Kept Ayrshire Cows
With just the odd Friesian**

Father always kept Ayrshire cows, but there was just the odd Friesian, which, when asked why, he would say tongue in cheek "Oh we just keep her at the end of the shed to wash the shed down with, you see its blue milk, no butterfat."

This was how The Beeches Farm looked years ago when we were kids. The building on the right in the back ground was where all the grain was stored in the loft and milled or crushed in the shed below, it also had the mangol pulper and straw chopper, from the days when it was all carried round the sheds to the cows.

Father and his neighbour sometime went up to Scotland to a breed sale and would buy about twenty incalf Ayrshire heifers between them, enough to fill a cattle lorry. We would get a phone call in advance about how many to expect and to prepare a be prepared for how many to be dropped in. Quite often the wagon would arrive back suitable shed for them to here before dad and his mate, at two in the morning. They put up in some digs over two nights and got home about lunch time the following day.

I recall that they had bought the first dehorned cattle in the area, and everyone was inquisitive to see these Ayrshire cattle with no horns. It was not long after that that he had the horns cut off all the cows and dehorned all calves as they were born. It was a gruesome job, and performed in the stalls where they were tied up, the vet tied string tightly round the base of the cows horns as a tourniquet, then used four foot shears to clip them off in one swift cut. It took two or three men to close the shears on the older cows, and on odd ones where they had cut close to the string, the string slipped off and blood spurted up in a fine spray up into the rafters of the cowshed. Talk about rivers of blood. After a day or two the wounds dried up, but it was noticeable that the cows that had always done the bullying now got a very soar head when they butted the others.

Father ran a dairy herd

Father ran a dairy herd,
of mainly Ayrshire cows,
These were housed traditionally,
tied in stalls in rows,
Brought down for milking,
had to be tied with a chain,
Each knew their own stall,
a left and a right contain.

Cows were used to standing,
to their own side of the stall,
They would part to let you
in between when you call,

A bowl full of corn,
and in with the bucket and stool,
Milked by hand while they're
eating good job when it's cool.

He was the first to try,
a newfangled milking machine,
Vacuum pipe was installed,
new motor and pump had to be,
Four buckets and spare,
four cows milked nice and clean,
This was quicker by far,
once the cows got used to routine.

Milk was cooled in the dairy,
with water from the well,
The dairy collected it every day,
had to be cool to sell,
The fridge a copper heat
exchanger hanging on the wall,
On top Dee shaped receiving pan,
milk we poured it all.

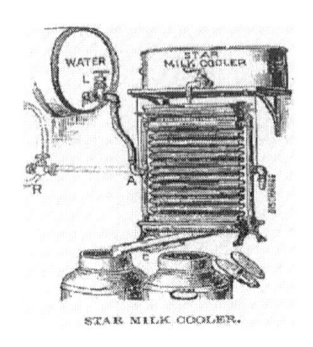

STAR MILK COOLER.

Well water runs on inside fridge,
milk run down outside,
Churns were filled for the dairy,
to a measured mark inside,

Labeled with where it's to go,
at one time went by train,
Now a lorry picks up churns,
a churn stand on the lane.

Thirty years he milked this
way, in churns milk was poured,
Restricted now by the number of
stalls, yields he did record,
Bulk tank came and a pipeline
too, milk tanker every day,
This took Father to retirement,
very modern to do it this way.

Father always reared all his heifer calves, and when AI first came about he used it on his best thirty cows and his own bull on the rest, the bull calves going off down to the market when old enough. Calves reared were started on their mother's milk and continued on cow's milk for a couple of weeks when gradually they were introduced onto gruel, which was mainly Linseed, and this had to be scalded before you could feed it to the calves. There was no powdered milk equivalent available then and gruel was the best option so the maximum milk could go to the dairy.

Linseed Gruel for Calves

Always reared our own
replacements, for the dairy herd,
Soon weaned off mother's milk,
linseed gruel prepared,
Gruel it had to be scalded,
to kill the enzymes off,
Otherwise the calves would
scour, and then begin to cough.

Just a week on full cow's milk,
started to feed them gruel
When they were a month old,
it was the only fuel,
Along with a bit of cow corn,
and a rack with meadow hay,
Reared, a bit potbellied,
when out they went on grass day.

A couple of years rearing and
growing, put them to the bull,
They will be replacements,
for the ones we have to cull,
Calved down at three years
old, to be a well grown cow,
Years in the dairy herd, good
feet and health allow.

As it has always been, there was dairy inspections, and these came when you least expected them, but the time to work seriously at cleaning up was usually on a very wet day.

The old white wash was scraped off the walls with garden hoe's along with the splashes of dried on cow muck, and a new coat of lime wash applied, this included the dairy where the milk was cooled and run into churns.

A Wet Day Job

On days when it's too wet work
outside, find a job indoors,
Grab hold of garden hoes,
scrape cowshed walls and floors,

A good soaking and scrubbing,
get the cow muck off,
Where the cows have splashed,
and had a dam good cough.

Out with a small tin bath,
bag of quick line pour,
Mix with water till a thin
paste, ten minutes stand before,
Brushed up the walls, with
a house brush soft,
Gleaming white and clean,
right up to the old hayloft

Spot check by the dairy
inspector, turn up out of the blue,
Just when you don't expect,
look at the sheds right through,
The milk house where milk
is cooled gets same job done,
Cows wary of the new décor,
inspectors' inspection won.

Molasses, has come back into fashion in the last twenty years or so, but when we were kid's father had a forty gallon drum in the corn shed on a block so he could run off some when it was needed. The drum was half used and thick with mill dust, and the lower small bung was only finger tight. We used to take this bung out and wait for the treacle to slowly ooze out and get fingers full of the stuff before replacing the bung

Black Molasses in the Barn

I Remember at the Beeches,
way back in the barn,
A great big forty gallon drum,
on a block away from harm,
It contained black molasses;
a good half of it was used,
With hot water mixed,
spread on oats when they're bruised.

Take the bung out and wait a bit,
for it to slowly flow,
We all liked to have a taste,
dad said it'd help us grow,
A finger full and then another,
it was lov-ely and sweet,
Left your hands all sticky,
you couldn't be discrete.

We had plenty over the time,
but still a lot unused,
Mother said it would move us,
but father he was amused,
He said a good clean out,
every now and then,
Would tone us up, and help
us all, to grow to big strong men.

———————-

A quarrel is like buttermilk, the more you stir it, the more sour it grows.
(Bolivian Proverb)

Chapter 12

Farm as if you'll Farm for Ever

This is a Massy Harris Binder like father had from 1938 to 1956 originally he pulled it with three shires then he had a clevis hitch put on the pole to shorten it and pulled it with his Standard Fordson.

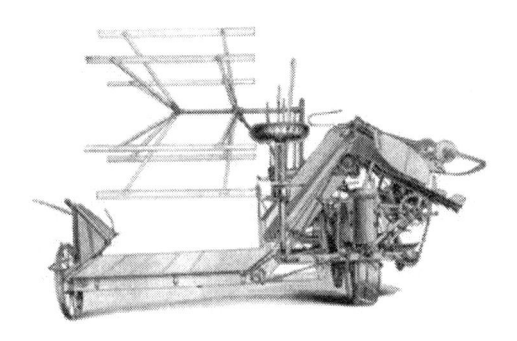

It's now nearing the time for harvest festivals in the villages all over the country, so I thought I would put in a few contributions of my own thoughts.

When you have time to stop and think about this world we live in, and the relatively short time that we have here, you begin to realize how the land controls almost everything. The land is a permanent feature that we only borrow for the time we have in this world, and everyone who looks after land, be it farm or garden has a responsibility to look after it for the next generation. As my father always said "Farm as if you'll farm forever, and live as if you'll die tomorrow".

From Nature's Larder it has come

You stand n think about the
crops, that took all year to grow,
The grass to graze the livestock,
and some we keep to mow,
To till the soil and sow the seed,
and keep the weeds at bay,
Through snow and frost, drought
and flood, warm sunshine on the way.

All the years we follow the
same seasons through the year,
Some extremes of weather,
of which we cannot interfere,
Nature has its way of telling,
who's in charge what is growing,
Gather what it gives you,
from seed that you've been sowing.

All things that you eat,
from nature's larder it has come,
Must be grateful for the harvest,
apples damsons and the plum,
Grain n' root crops, beef n' pork,
lamb and chicken are grown,
On the land that we look after,
seeds of life that we have sown.

It's only lent us while were here,
for generations you can see,
The mark on land and farms let
the fields and hedgerow be,
All people who on earth do come,
respect the soil and plants,
Were only here for a short time,
its beauty always enchants.

You can if you like put the following verse to the tune of "We plough the fields and scatter" but then we must not try to improve too much on the old traditional words, The vicar had a look and said no, we'll stick to the traditional verses, but I tried.

Harvest Celebration

Completion of the harvest,
is a time to celebrate,
Leaves on trees are yellowing,
around the whole estate,
Barns and bins are full to
bursting, for winter now is here,
In olden days it was the same,
to grow still takes a year.

A lot more hand work then,
more men worked upon the land,
Ploughed with horses and acre
a day, seed was sown by hand,
Good rotation of all the crops,
kept most weeds at bay,
At harvest stood sheaves up in stooks,
for two church bells they must stay.

Bays n ricks were built, threshed
as needed through the year,
Wheat went to the mill be ground,
flour for bread revere,
Oats to feed the cattle and horses,
some for porridge bound,
To feed the men and families who,
work the land all year round.

Mechanized and fewer men,
but crops still grow the same,
Sunshine and warmth in the spring,
showers to grow good crops the aim,
In nature nothing really changes,
seasons come and go,
To keep us on the land we love,
food for everyone we grow.

  This is an old tree that struggles into life each spring, its hollow and frail full of insects, and at one time the gate used to hang on it and the barbed wire stapled to it. The cows use it as a rubbing post, although it is fairly sheltered from any high winds, and also lost most of its canopy it still stand stubbornly on from one year to the next.

We have a poor old Alder tree

We have a poor old Alder tree,
standing by a gate,
Been there a long time,
wire and rails locate,
Grown in the fence line
and now matured,
Nails and hinges in the trunk,
below the bark obscured.

As the branches break away,
and rot gets in its core,
It becomes hollow down the
middle, breaks away some more,
All one side is open now,
right down to the ground,
Still clad with bark on three sides,
inside insects abound.

Its canopy is in full leaf,
but a skeleton of what it was,
Wonder how it still stands,
the rubbing cattle draws,
All gnarled and knobbly,
from the years of damage
A sort of beauty in its old age,
time has took its ravage.

What a subject for someone to paint, the photograph was taken well over a year ago, and still it stands right now September 2008.

It will too dangerous to try and chain saw the lower five foot, it has old gate hinges, old horse shoe hammered in for slip rails, six inch nails that held oak rails. Umpteen staples and wire were strained up to it, the barbed wire all embedded under the bark. I put some in myself and also saw most of them disappear over the years.

A harvest of peace is produced from a seed of contentment
American Proverb

Chapter 13

How we lived in the Old House

Insulations none existent,
big jumper you must ware,
Half-timbered single brick,
few inches plaster of horse hair,
Frosty weather glistens inside,
a fridge you could compare,
Roof half filled with starling's
nests, built up over the years.

Kitchens the warmest place,
coal fire in big old range,
Heats the oven and boils,
the kettle on the chimney crane,
Boils the taters and stew,
toast the bread on a fork,
From ceiling hangs a cloths
drier, lifts and lowers on cord.

Bedroom bove the kitchen,
only room upstairs warm,
Usually the kids have this room,
that is always the norm,
Other rooms are chilled and cold,
cool in summer though,
This is how we lived them
days, kids now will never know.

Old iron bedstead web with steel,
straw mattress on the top,
Then feather mattress covered
with a white sheet she'd pop,

Mother made a groove up this,
dropped us into bed,
Sheet two blankets n eiderdown,
feather pillow lay ya head.

Best front room not often used,
too posh to use every day,
Used over Christmas and party's,
best crockery out on display,
Fathers roll top desk in there,
his bills and letters wait to pay,
Always locked cus of cash in
their, he always had last say.

Now heating was a big open fire,
ingle nook chimney above,
Logs as long as ya can lift,
one end on the fire to shove,
The bigger the fire, bigger
the draught across the floor,
The heat goes up the chimney,
fresh air comes in under the door.
(in the form of draught)

A cellar beneath front room,
brick steps leading down,
Couple of vents to the garden,
mesh with weeds overgrown,
Air circulation its not good,
and musty damp and wet,
Timber in the floor above,
weak and springy pose a threat.

A room with settlass all way
round, there to salt the pig,
Been used now twice a year,
doesn't look so big,

Salt has drawn up the brickwork,
all through to outside
Bricks are flaking and rotting,
replaced section bricks decide.

Mother kept a big tin bath,
hung on a nail outside back door,
Brought it in to the hearth,
a kettle and big jug she pour,
Youngest first then nother kettle,
warm it agen for the second,
Cold night our steaming
bodies, hot crisp towel it beckoned.

We kids lived in the big kitchen,
in bedroom top back stairs,
Long old sofa under the window,
father had his own armchair,
Big old peg rug in front of the fire,
we played and sat on that,
Large old radio in the window,
then hurray first tele in front we sat.

Feathers Floating Round the Light

With four lads in the house it was obvious that discipline was going play a big part of growing up. Father always wore bracers and had no belt thank goodness, but he wasn't shy of using his slipper.

Chasing kids was not very high on his list of things to do. It did not help that we had a front stairs and back stairs, and also our bedroom was above the kitchen, so bumping and banging jumping on and off the dressing table onto the bed and sometimes missing, made the white wash flake off the ceiling over dad's chair.

White wash was what the cowsheds and dairy were painted with, and also used in the farm house kitchen over the years. Its burnt lime mixed with water and brushed on the walls or in the case of the kitchen ceiling, and its added to every year or so and builds up to a brittle thickness that can't stand vibration.

Father Used His Slipper

Father always used his slipper,
when we were being naughty,
But we were quick and dodged
about, for he was over forty,
He chased upstairs into our
room, he thought he'd got us now,
We dived under both the beds,
to reach us he dint know how.

Looking back he never hurt us,
slapped a slipper on the floor,
The noise and shouting gave
us speed, we never had before,
Beeches had two lots of stairs,
up one and down the other,
Dad soon got out of puff;
and shouted for our mother.

A couple of smacks across the
bum, and on he put his slipper,
And told us off when we did
wrong, but never was he bitter,

Respect was what he taught us,
and elders must not cheek,
Listen to what you're being told,
with P's and Q's must speak.

Pillow fights at bed time,
when we should be fast asleep,
Jumping high up to the ceiling,
were not counting sheep,
Our room was buv the kitchen,
and noise he couldn't stand,
Heard him rushing up the stairs,
for piece and quite demand.

He came in, were in bed,
feathers floating round the light,
Pretending were asleep, bulb
still swinging from the fight,
Settle down we had to now,
if he came up a second time,
We'd all be in trouble, twas
the stairs that he had to climb.

He had done a hard days work,
and had settled in his chair,
Running up the stairs at night,
enough to make him swear,
Slipper slapping on the treads,
we knew what he had got,
So fast asleep pretend to be,
looked like he'd lost the plot.

Not until just before dawn do people sleep best; not until people get old do they become wise.
 Chinese Proverb

Chapter 14

"Trotters"

We watched when we were kids,
Fingers in our ears,
Then bang the butcher shot him,
cut its throat mid tears.

I never knew who owned the pig bench but it went round all the village to whoever had got a pig ready for killing.

I Remember Killing the Pig

About once a year the butcher called,
for to kill a pig,
Scrubbed off the pig bench,
it was heavy and big,
Don't know whose it was,
but around the village it went,
To lay the pig on when it's killed,
four wooden legs all bent.

Starve the pig from day before,
empty belly they need,
Then the butcher prepares his tools,
then the pig to lead,
By a noose round his snout,
mid squealing protest struggle,
Took three men to lift on bench,
to hold it on they grapple.

We watched all this when we were
kids, fingers in our ears,
Then bang the butcher shot him,
and cut its throat mid tears,
It happened fast, the kids will
learn; catch the blood in bucket,
Kicking stopped, and bucket full,
into pantry put it.

Very hot water poured all over,
and scrape the hair all off,
He scalded the hooves,
with a hook ripped the hoof clean off,
This was worst he opened it up,
all put into the barrow,
Save the heart, liver kidneys,
same sequence always follow.

Then with a "tree", like a big
clothes hanger, lifted pig to beam,
Left to set almost week, butcher
returns, to watch were keen,.
Head comes off to make the
brawn, boiled in a great big pot,
The rest is quartered, for to salt
down, onto the setlas brought.

Fresh pork saved to use right now,
take the neighbours some,
Other do the same as well, almost
every month a treat become,
Two hams in muslin bags are hung,
on hook in pantry cool,
The bacon too is done the same,
enough to make you drool.

Mother makes the faggots and
black puddings from the blood,
Nothings ever wasted, fat is
rendered down, scratching's good,
Lard for frying and cooking,
stored all in big stone jars,
Lined up in the pantry,
all the work done, by our poor old m'a.

Mother would not kill off a hen that was young and healthy, or an old one that was laying, it was always a bare arsed one that was almost spent out. They were never allowed to die, she would get them just before that get it plucked and in the pot never having time to go cold.

I remember Mothers Mid-Week Chicken Dinner

In mid-week we often had,
"chicken" for our dinner,
Tough old hen more soup than
meat, always it was a winner,
So after breakfast mother went,
to feed the laying hens,
On her way she would note,
the one who's still in pens.

If it looked as if not laying,
she would ring its neck,
Hang it in the coal shed,
all flap and no more peck.
Pulling on the old tea cozy,
well down over her ears,
An old mac kept for this job,
doesn't matter how it appears.

Feathers and the fluff do fly,
and also mites do run,
This is why she's well covered up,
as it is so often done,
With the newspaper on the table,
to be drawn it is now ready,
Out with good sharp knife,
off with legs and neck all bloody.

Nick below the parson's nose,
hand the guts she pulls the lot,
Saves the heart and gizzard,
also neck to make the stock,
Into the pot this tough old hen,
no time for it to go cold,
Steamed for a good two hours,
till lid is hot to hold.

Into the pot goes all the veg,
and a heap of part boiled taties,
Given another half hour simmering,
before it hits the platters,
We all come in for dinner time,
lunch to someone posh,
Plates piled up, our bellies to fill,
we loved our chicken nosh.

In the kitchen at the Beeches the kitchen floor sloped from east to west, with the fire place range on the south side. (Get the picture) It was a blue brick floor the same as in the stable, and the walls were the bare bricks painted, one colour usually green half way up and a lighter colour round the top usually green with white washed ceiling. To the side of the chimney breast was mother's new Jackson electric cooker, where she cooked the bacon or porridge in a mornings before the range had properly got going. I remember the porridge would lift the lid with cooking and spill down the sides welding the pan to the cooker, Porridge had to simmer for an hour just to cook, no instant heat and eat, like the two minuet porridge of today, and they were rolled raw oats.

To the other side of the chimney breast was a built in cupboard with a half bottom door and half top door stable door style if you like to call it. There was some hot pipes running through this cupboard and the Kellogg Cornflakes were kept to keep dry, along with the sugar and flour. This was a cupboard that was often raided by mice but they disappeared up into the ceiling following the pipes. To the north side was a large cupboard with four draws at the bottom, and two big opening doors on the top half, on the top shelf dad kept his pipe and bacca, though he did not us it that regular? Us kids tried his pipe out one night with dried tea leaves, cus we could-na find any bacca. We all had one good drag and it literally spun us off our feet, and I never ever smoked again, perhaps a good lesson learned early.

Also on the top shelf was the shot gun cartridges, quite a few boxes, stacked as these were used to get our rabbit dinner once a week, and occasionally a poached pheasant. In the rest of the shelves were the bottles and jar that had been opened and part used like jams and pickles and that posh word for salt vinegar and pepper, a cruet.

The Kitchen Floor it sloped.

I remember when we were kids,
kitchen floor it sloped,
Sat down at meal times,
mother to top end coped,
Kitchen table vinyl cloth,
also it did tilt,
Father down one side,
safe from anything that spilt.

Always there is one,
who's clumsy as a kid,
Put him at the lower end,
own mess he is amid,
Tip the water over,
or a cup of tea,
It runs down the table,
straight into his knee.

Four of us took it in turns,
not to be so clumsy,
Other three would laugh,
all sitting dry and cozy,
A dam good lesson that it was,
with insta-tant results,
Chair at the lower end,
reserved for bumble foots.

———————

We had visiting mice in the house from time to time but mother was crafty, and they did not last long, She always had a couple of mouse traps and a lump of stale cheese pressed onto them, being thrifty the same piece of cheese would often catch more than one mouse.

A Mouse in the Cupboard

Sitting in the kitchen one night,
by the kitchen fire,
Mother knitting father reading,
us lads getting tired.
Then we heard a rustling,
in the cupboard by chimney breast,
It was Kellogg's corn flakes
trickling, a mouse the little pest.

He had sat and chewed a hole,
right through cornflake box,
Found food for his belly,
where our mother keeps her stocks,
He disappeared up round some
pipes, still the flakes they fell,
Keeping warm and well fed,
if we find him give him hell.

Set the mouse trap on the shelf,
loaded up with cheese,
For this it would attract him,
one bite make him sneeze,
Spring will slap him on the head,
teach him not to steal,
Wasteful little blighter,
to us it was our meal.

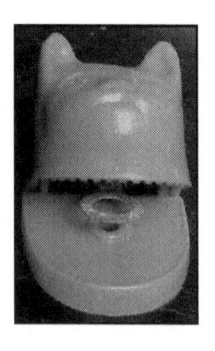

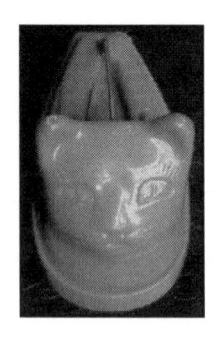

Here's a fancy mouse trap if you like

Quotation
A crust eaten in peace is better than a banquet partaken in anxiety.
Aesop (620BC-560BC)

Chapter 15

The Village wheelwright and his Family

They had a little grey Fergy tractor, which was used to cart the muck out to the field in winter, and in the summer, they would mow the meadows for hay.

This is the White Cottage the smallholding which was also the wheelwrights shop. On the extreme right is the workshop and hay barn

The White Cottage.
(Or the Smallholding)

This cottage opposite the pub was occupied by Mr. and Mrs. Clark. It was a small holding of about forty acres, as on all the farms on the estate, it had some close land, and some on the meadows down the Moss lane, and some over the railway down the Moor lane. This house had only one main room, and a scullery, then a lean-to on the back of the house, this was used as a dairy to cool and store the milk churns overnight, until the milk man came the following morning. Upstairs it had two bedrooms, and the only privy was a little brick and tile loo, under a bush, down the garden path. In this house they brought up a family of six children.

The new workshop that Jim and Bill built is on the left, the two chimneys above were the two new council houses that they lived in later in life. The two chimneys in the centre are that of the village shop, (looking from its rear), and below on the right was the original workshop that their old man used from the 1900's

Old Harry Clark, their father, I can only just remember, he was not a very tall man, and quite round in his later years. He was a wheelwright by trade, and worked in a low tin roofed shed down below the wooden pole hay barn. He was a man who enjoyed a joke, and quite mischievous in a nice way. It was said that when bagged fertilizer first came out, Charlie Finnimore, [of Yews Farm] sent a new man to spread it on the meadows under the Ashes Wood. It turned out he had spread it on one of Harry's small fields down there. Later Mr. Finnimore realized the mistake, and went round to see Harry for recompense, only to be told very politely that he did not want it, and that he could send the man down the following morning to pick it up again, as he did not mind at all!.

Mrs. Clark, Harry's wife, could only just get about, and getting a very old lady, like Harry she was quite round, and had her own chair by the fire where she could easily reach the kettle, without having to move. In fact as a child I was amazed that when Mrs. Clark was sitting down she seemed to have no knees. Her part in the carpentry business, over the years, was to line the coffins that Harry made, for the local people, who were then buried in St Chad's churchyard. They had six children, Henry [called Harry] the oldest, Jim, Bill the youngest, and three daughters in between.

Henry worked for the post office as a postman, and travelled to work in a little old Austin 7 car, the one that had a straight up windscreen and a starting handle permanently out in front.

Henry was the smallest of all the family, and walked with a heavy limp; this was due to him having a short leg and had a boot with a four or five inch sole. Henry lived with his wife Nell in the cottage next to Cooksland Farm gate, on the other side of the lane was a small garage for his car. Nell worked up at Cooksland House for Major Eld, and her father lived in a small room, or lean-to, on the end of a house on the end of Smithy Lane. He was Bill Ecclestone a very old man when I was a child; he helped around the different farms when needed. His worn-out body seamed to lean forward, almost forming a loop under his bracers, where his chest had been. He wore corduroy trousers that were tied below the knee with string, and old boots that had worn out laces. The shirts worn in them days all had loose collars, his shirt at work had no collar or stud to hold the neck hole together, and looked as though it had seen many washes (and missed a few as well). He lived an independent life in his small room, but well looked after by his daughter Nell.

Jim was the tallest of the family, and when married

lived in the second house up the Coton lane [turn left at the west end of the village second house on the right]. This had a craft, [Crofters have crafts- small field] where he kept hens and reared a few pigs, it had two pig sty's. He worked as carpenter for the estate along with Eric Kilford who was the builder bricklayer; Eric built up Kilfords the Building firm and employed quite a lot of men. Jim took over from his father, when his father became too old to continue, having learned all the skills needed to become a wheelwright, and all the traditional tools that had built up over the years for that trade.When the Cumbers council houses were built, in the 1950s, Jim moved into No10, and Bill moved into No9, right opposite the farm and workshop. By this time Jim was full time, having taken over from "The old Chap". Jim and Bill built a new workshop, with double doors that would lock, a great deal higher and bigger than the one the old chap used. A complete farm wagon could be built and painted all indoors, and a good deal lighter as well.

As I said Jim was tall, all of six foot, but I expect that working all his earlier days in low cottages, and always ducking his head, he carried his head slightly forward, giving him a slight hump on his shoulders. (Not quite as tall as he should be). They all had caps on in them days, and Jim had his pipe always in his teeth, not always lit. It was St Julian tobacco, that he smoked, and I got as much pleasure, from the smell of the smoke, as he did smoking it.

You get the ambiance of a room or workshop when you walk into it, so you did from Jim's workshop, with the smoke from his pipe, or the new cut oak shavings, or the fresh new paint when he's finishing off a job. His pipe spent so much time, in his teeth, that it wore his teeth away in that one place, to the extent that he could clench his teeth tightly, and the pipe would still hang comfortably. In normal talk, he would talk with the pipe in place. But if some cussing was to be done, it would be a prodding motion with the pipe in his hand. But more often than not it was tongue in cheek cussing. (Enough about the pipe).

It was always a big joke when Jim and his wife Minnie, went on holiday for a week to the seaside with friends. Minnie would have Jim move all the furniture, to dust and polish, "even behind the bl---- wardrobes had to be cobwebbed" he went on, in case someone had to look in, while they were away. Minnie was a big friend of my mothers, and was very proud of her new house, number 10 The Cumbers. She was also keen on her flowers garden, and front lawn. Jim had to do the lawn mowing and dug and planted the veg patch. His comment to these jobs was "Why didn't they build the B motorway across my front lawn, or at least tarmac it" he went on, "I could sweep it off and paint it green each spring and save all this work."

    Bill, the youngest of the family, looked after the cows. Up until the 1950s they were hand milked, and then they had their first milking machine. Then followed a few years later with a bulk milk tank, they stopped picking milk up in churns shortly after that. Bill had 14 cows that was the maximum that the sheds would hold. They were well looked after, and heavy milkers. They were always turned out for the night onto the craft opposite the Holly Bush Pub. During the day they went down through the ford, to the banky field at the end of Moor lane, or the field at the top of the road bank on the right. At the ford cows from other herds came from all directions. Village Farm cows came down the bank to the ford the up the Moor lane, Church Farm cows went down the same way as Bills. On the village green, Green Farm cows would be going out, and also Yews Farm cows went across the green to the Moss Lane.
    On a few occasions Bill would have to encourage his

cows to move across the path of another herd, or sometimes meet another herd head on. He always had a long nut stick, and always on his bike when on the road with the cows, and when a problem like this came up, he would get off his bike, and gently tap his cows on through the opposing "team". He rarely lost any or picked any extra up, the cows knowing their own fields or sheds.

In his younger days Bill was in the village cricket team, often he was wicket keeper, then when in batting he would hit and run, and really liven the proceedings up, scoring some very quick runs, or getting himself or his colleague run out. The cricket square was in the middle of the present village football field. It was a football field then as well. During the week the cricket square was fenced off, and Bills cows would graze round it.

Always a joker he would examine a person's ploughing, to see if it was strait. If it was one of us younger ones, and it was crooked, he would be relentless in telling anyone who would listen, as to how many dead rabbits he had picked up. Telling them how they had broken their necks, running round the bends in the furrows. Another wheeze he had was when someone had spent a day working hard at cleaning or sweeping up, he would say "That looks better, which bit have you done ?", then watch for the reaction, then laugh. Only a small man, he had a job to reach the floor when astride his bike, and with his Woodbine lit, and his nut stick across his handle bars, set off promptly at three fifteen to fetch the cows in. As long as everyone else was at the regular time, the herds would not clash.

They had a little grey Fergy tractor, which was used to cart the muck out to the field in winter, and in the summer, they would mow the meadows for hay. Then when they wanted timber for carpentry, they would be off down to Henry Venables timber yard on the tractor, sometimes for wide elm boards, still with the bark edges, for trailer floors, or oak for making gates, or timber for making a coffin. If anyone died in the village, Jim and Bill would be called. I remember one occasion when Bill was not available, Jim called my brother and I to help him lay out a neighbour who had died that morning.

The first thing we were asked to do was to lift the pantry door off its hinges, and put it on the table. Then we helped lift the deceased onto the door to lay her out, this was a normal procedure as there is not much room in a lot of cottages, and pantry door or scullery door had hinges like a gate, and could easily be lifted off. When Jim was walking off down the village, with a long notched stick in his hand, we knew he was off to measure a body for the coffin. People did not have long measuring tapes, as we have now, so a long measuring stick was used. (Carpenters usually had a wooden two foot rule).

If you are a person living in one of the Seighford cottages, you may never realize what your old pantry door had been used for, besides blocking a hole in the wall.

After having got the measurements required from the body, Jim would proceed to make the coffin. This would take all afternoon, and he would work into the evening to get the job done. On occasions Eric Bennion would call with his car, to transport the coffin to the deceased's house, discreetly covered with a blanket. His car had a large carrier rack on the back the right size.

I heard a story about Eric, carting a coffin about on the back of his car, when food rationing was on. There were strict restrictions enforced by the police, usually by the local bobby on a bike based at Great Bridgeford the next village. Eric, Jim and Bill had to move a pig that had just been killed at one of their houses, to someone who wanted it, but shouldn't have it because of rationing. So the obvious way was in a coffin, covered up on the back of Eric's car, and at night. I believe they passed the police but were never suspected.

Of course all the men of working age at that time, were in the "Home Guard" based in Great Bridgeford village hall. No end of contraband food exchange hands without a ration book in sight, not all of them worked on farms or were farmers.

Never discourage anyone........ Who continually makes progress, no matter how slow
 ato (347BC-427 BC)

Chapter 16

Verse to the Wheelwright's Shop

These men Jim and Bill were the same age and era as my parents, they both retired in 1985 when there was no more call for traditional wooden carts and wagons, metal gates were being peddled by Gypo's in Transit trucks, and the tractors were matched up to three ton hydraulic tipping trailers. The age of the "thimble cart" (a tipping cart with shafts and five foot wooden hooped wheels) some of these had been converted with a tractor drawbar, but they only carried just less than a ton.

The Wheelwrights' Shop Seighford

Wheelwrights' shop, was run,
By Jim Clark and his brother Bill,
A wonderful smell new sawn oak,
Varnish glue and paint as well,
Soft under foot with sawdust,
And shavings that drop from his plane,
Inside of its door painted like rainbow,
From cleaning paint brush again.

The timber he needed he fetched,
Henry Venables Castletown saw mill,
Oak, elm, beech and ash,
All were rough sawn to plane and drill,
Wheelbarrows carts and gates,
And wagon wheels, re made or repaired,
Some that his father had
made years before,
There was nothing to compare.

On the way home from school,
We'd call to see what he was making,
And watch its progress each day,
How and when and why we were asking,
From the first piece rough timber,
Laid on his trestles to start,
To when he'd finished painting it,
Name of the farm lettered and smart.

Jim he was tall with slight stoop,
He was broad on his back and shoulders,
His cap was square on his head,
Cept tipped back a bit when he ponders
always a smile with his
pipe in his mouth,
He loved to have a natter,
It wore a groove in his teeth,
And wobbled about when he chattered.

With bib and brace overalls,
And laced up leather tipped boots,
Short overall jacket hangs open,
All washed and cleaned like his suit,
Minie his wife took pride in his turnout,
Never a scruff at all has he been,
She loved her garden not like Jim,-
Tarmac it over and paint it green.

Bill kept twelve cows and some calves,
Cowshed on the yard by the road,
Jim helped with the milking, and mucking out to the
ruck he barrowed,
Milk was carried up to their White
House, the lean to a dairy it was,
Three or four milk churns
Rolled to the kerb,
Hand over hand without pause.

Bill was quite short and stocky,
And smoked his woodbines all day,
Permanent smile and a grin,
Always a joke and a pranks did he play,
He was in village cricket team,
Wild batter and runner was he,
Other batter often got run out,
Umpire he'd decry with loud plea.

He'd gather his cows on his bike,
Six o'clock in the morning with woodbine,
Afternoon milking was three thirty,
Back to the field at five for bovine,
He had to go down to the Floshes,
Count his heifer on the meadows,
During the day he helped in the shop,
He painted the trailers and barrows.

At dinner time mid-day both crossed,
The road their houses retire,
For Bill he had an hours sleep,
On the heath in front of the fire,
He was the youngest of large family,
And slept cause there wasn't a chair
This habit remained with him,
Curled up on the rug and comfy there.

Jim he drove their Fergy tractor,
On Satdee morning carted the muck,
They both loaded onto the cart by hand,
In field they made a ruck,
In the summer they mowed their hay,
Bill he rode on the mower,
clearing the blockage, pulling
long leaver, that to lift and lower.

Jim he also made the coffins,
For any villagers who died,
He was the first to know,
He lay them out and measure applied,
In one small cottage with not much
room, he lifted off the pantry door,
With no one else about he asked,
For me to help lift body off the floor.

This was the first I'd seen dead body,
And shook me dam well ridged,
Out with his tape and pencil,
See how big to make the coffins image,
With his pipe in his mouth still puffin,
He talked to the person by name,
Eggcup under the head, big toes tied together,
Hands on chest what a shame.

Coffins he made in the evening,
The tapping his hammer till late,
His mother and wife they lined it,
Now ready to load in his mate,
Bill in the meantime he dug the grave,
Down to the previous coffin,
It'd been a few years since I was down
hear, bump with the spade to waken.

Jim and his father made many cart wheels,
Hubs spokes and fellows and all,
The hubs were made out of elm,
Spokes and fellows were ash I recall,
When they were ready were
Wheeled to the blacksmith,
He made the hot metal band,
To shrink round the fellows forthwith.

As the years went by, and cheap metal
gates, trailers for tractors came in,
This cut down his work fancy gates did
he make, along with repairs within,
They both retired as age caught up,
The wheelwrights shop it closed,
An era had passed when they sold up,
Into history they were reposed.

———————-

Half our life is spent trying to find something to do with the time, we have rushed through our life trying to save
    Will Rogers (1879-1935)

Chapter 17

Grandma Always had a Very Best' Strong Float (1920)

This is a story about my grandma, who worked against all odds to rear her brood of nine kids, and some of the things she got up to, and realize where I get my temper from, though it takes a lot of provoking these days to wind me up.

Mothers younger days.
In his late teens father got his first rented fields, about 12 acres with a small shed where he bought his first sow, then swapped it for his first cow and started milking, this was adjacent to his own fathers farm, where just a few hundred yard down the road on another farm where my mother was born and lived.

Mother was brought up on the farm at Coton Clanford, she was one of 9 children and was a twin, they were the 7th and 8th born and reared by their elder sisters, grandma was widowed not long after the youngest was born. It was a struggle for her to run the farm and rear such a big family, it was not uncommon for her to be seen with a pair of work horses ploughing, and doing all other laborious work that had to be done about the farm, helped of course by some of older children and a faithful bachelor cousin Charlie, who stepped in and stayed with her for the rest of his life.

The Chapel that they attended every Sunday, was situated just down the road from the farm, where, grandma played the organ and sometimes conducted the services, it was compulsory for all the family to go twice every Sunday. It's a very small building holding no more than 20 seated but at times many more would pack into its small room. Very loud and enthusiastic singing was the main aim of the venue; later in life mother was in the Seighford School and St. Chad's church choir.

This is the old Coton Clanford Chapel as it is today, it's now used by the local scouts as a HQ, but when it was used as a chapel it had seating for about twenty and a pulpit and an organ that had to be treddled, also a small vestry at the back (lean to at the far end). Still got the original iron railings along the front.

There are three foundation stone built into the front wall one each side of the porch and one above, but they are that badly weathered the sandstone lettering is now unreadable.

Grandma, mothers mother (Mother had lost her father and father had lost his mother,) was a very tall and robust woman, about six foot and sixteen stone, not a person to be ignored. When I knew her as a little lad she was getting bent with age and nowhere near her youthful height, She always wore a hat and a huge hat pin, normally black and a black dress almost ankle length and a dark three quarter length coat with big pockets, and to top it off when going to chapel or visiting she always had her fox fur. This hung around her shoulders with a clip on its jaw to make it look as though it was biting its own tail. The foxes eyes were bright and very piercing, and as it hung over the back of our chair at home one night father was manipulating its head round the settee just as the cat was purring round the other way, when the cat saw the piercing eyes glaring at it, the fox jumped forward . Need I say the fox lost a lot of fur and father got cussed in no uncertain terms, amid peals of laughter from all the family?

Grandma always had a very strong 'best' float to go to town in, most people had traps or gigs, rather light and delicate in build and lightly sprung for comfort, but she had to have something that would take at least a good proportion of the family. Like car drivers now they had "road rage" and aggressive drivers as well in them days. I fear to tell you that grandma was one of these.

A long standing feud with a person who used the same road to Stafford and back, found themselves using it on the same day, on a very narrow section of road along Butterbank, but they were going in opposite directions. Neither would hold back to let the other through, so with a quick flap of the reins grandma increased speed, and rushed the gap, she set her jaw, and clenched some of her teeth, her hat pulled well down and pinned in all directions as usual . With one wheel on the grass and a steady eye for the road beyond she got through, slowed the cob to a trot she never looked back. If she had looked back as some of her family helpers did, she would have seen a trap still moving along the road slowly, the driver on his back side in the middle of the road, and the axle and wheels of the above mentioned vehicle twisted and half way over the hedge. The hubs of the respective vehicles had met with great force, grandma having the greater weight in wheels and cart contents, lost only a scuff to the paint, the other almost totally destroyed.

Mother started school with her twin sister at the age

of 3 in 1912 at Seighford school walking just over a mile past Oldfords farm and across the footpath that comes down the cumbers (a field south of the school) the footpath coming through the blacksmiths garden a cottage by the side of the school, where the school caretaker lived. The head master then was Boss Plant and the infant school teacher was Miss Pye who taught me to write in the same class some 30 yrs. later. From my own recollection of Miss Pye, she was getting quite old when she taught me, but she was quite slim and elegant, old fashion in her dress always wore her hat when cycling to school on her sit-up and beg bike. It had a heavy looking chain case a large basket on the front, and carrier on the back where she strapped her rain coat, and on the rear wheel it had protective cords threaded from the mud guard to the spindle in a fan shape to stop her dress and coat catching in the wheel.

She taught us to write in big bold sweeping loops then later how to join them up , I notice even now there are some people, taught by Miss Pye, who write very similar to each other, including mother and myself. Miss pyre retired and lived on to over a hundred, she lived in the same house at Doxey all her life.

On leaving school mother went into "service" in a big house up the Stone road at Stafford to bring in the essential money to help keep the family at home surviving. It was a very lean time for farming and not enough work at home to keep them all in full time employment. Grandma always said she looked forward to Sunday mornings as there was no postman to bring unwelcome bills.

It was around this time father bought a motor bike, an old Valasett belt driven machine and he and mother used to travel the area on a Sunday afternoon when she was off work but he had to be home for evening milking. Mother being an absolute wiz at knitting, knitted him his only pair of gloves he ever had for on the bike. They had to be specially made as he had lost two finger on one hand in an accident clearing the blade of a horse drawn mowing machine when living with his uncle. In all my life I had never known him own another pair of gloves.

Grandma's Shopping Day

This happened along Butterbank Nr Stafford (around 1920)

My old grandma she had nine kids,
She took them all to chapel,
Twice every Sunday she played
the organ,
Till rafters they did rattled,
Squashed in and full it seated twenty;
All singing load and hearty,
This was mothers training,
a life of hymns and chorus cheery.

Grandma was a keen driver,
Of the horse and float,
and when she went to town,
Two pins in hat and on with coat,
Load up the younger kids to help,
All singing in the back,
to get supplies to last the week,
Then the whip she cracked.

A fine old trot the cob strode out;
To town not long it took,
sell some eggs and butter,
Done the shopping no kid forsook,

Halfway home the road got narrow,
Another trap was bearing down,
Twas a neighbour who had a row,
And grandma put on a frown.

Grandma pulled her hat down tight,
And then she set her jaw,
She was not the one to give way,
And flip the horse some more,
The float hub cap it struck the trap,
And knocked the wheels from under,
Not looking back she kept on track,
And home with face like thunder.

In modern terms you would say,
That this was only road rage,
No one he could complain to,
His trap in pieces sat in rampage,
Grandma upright stood six foot,
And no one crossed her twice,
Count her hat pins as a gauge,
To see if it's safe to ask advice.

Her farm house was heated with coal and logs, and lit by paraffin lamp and candles, then when Grandma got modern, she had a wireless powered by an accumulator.

(**Accumulator** — *a glass battery with two terminals on the top, four screw caps on the cells, and a cord loop to carry it about, it was taken to the local garage to be charged up)*

The Cast Iron Range

In years gone by when
Cooking was done,
Cooked with coal and logs,
In pots upon,
then the cast iron range,
Came into use,
in house and cottage,
all black and spruce.

Blazing dancing flame,
reaching up and back,
To chimney hood it's drawn,
all sooty and black,
Had two ovens,
with big black knobs,
To cook for the family,
and bake the cobs.

Kettle on a hook swung
over the fire,
Always on the boil
till tea we desire,
Pots on the side to
boil the taters,
Pan on the trivet fry
bacon for the platters

A toasting fork, to toast
the stale bread,
Hung on a nail in
the homestead,
Nothing was wasted,
all was used up,
Meat boiled off bones,
made broth to sup.

For years and years these
ranges were used,
The lectric came in,
and every one enthused,
Cooked with a switch,
on the wall turned on,
Off and all went cold, missed
the faithful range be gone.

(Cliché)
Grandmother used to say, **"The black cat is always the last one off the fence"** I have no idea what she meant, but at one time, it was undoubtedly true.
Solamon Short

Chapter 18

To Farming College I was sent

Tipped us all out into a huge rhubarb patch, the clumsy driver was the head of department, that cart was decommissioned shortly afterwards as too unstable for the job. A story of how it happened, and some of the highlights of my year at college

This is a picture the old Hall, the windows on the second and third floors were the dormitories for the male students. One hot night one of the lads moved his bed out onto the narrow balcony above the French windows, (good job he got out of bed on the correct side). On one occasion an item of girls' underwear was flown from the top of one of the very tall fir trees just on this lawn, no one dare fetch them down, or admit to putting them up there in the first place.

Rodbaston Farming College 1958

In my late teens it was arranged that I would have twelve months at Rodbaston Farm College, this was when I lost touch with Eileen, and it was to be over sixteen years before we met again.

It was a residential course and I only got home every other weekend if father had time on a Saturday afternoon to fetch me and take me back on a Sunday evening. Some of the inmates took the course seriously and a few other younger ones fooled about and learned very little.

It was about this time that the first combines were just beginning to appear in our area and the very first sugar beet harvesters were being tried out at the college while I was there, both machines revolutionized farming, by eliminating a lot of very heavy hand work. Another machine just coming out then was the crop sprayer and there were just about two options of spray to go into it. One dealt with thistles and docks in corn, the other did thistles and buttercups in grassland. There were no annual weeds to deal with to speak of in them days as everyone followed a strict rotation. Spraying allowed continuous corn cropping (Mono cropping) which in turn encouraged annual weeds. The latest tractors were also tried out and demonstrated at Rodbaston some of the largest were over a hundred horse power, and with these bigger tractors came ploughs to match them and other cultivation equipment.

In the livestock section the first milking parlors were just appearing where the cows came to the milking units and not the other way round as in the old cowshed milking, and cow cubicles were just invented. The college still milked cows in a double cowshed tied up by self-closing yolks.

On the social side of my stay at Rodbaston there were quite a few memorable incidents. Every so often we (the students) would be invited to another college or a visiting college would be invited to join us at Rodbaston for a social evening. As you may realize there was a great demand for baths, not many showers about in those days. Those in first or just early had the maximum hot water, the second lot the hot water system could not keep time with the demand and had cold baths, so as disgruntled students are, displeasure was shown in the testing of the drains around the student accommodation. (The maintenance man had been trying to clear a blocked drain all day.) This was achieved by the filling of all the baths (about ten as I recall) full to the brim with cold water and all the wash basins, then at a given signal all the plugs were pulled, all the toilets flushed as many time as possible. On observing the manhole covers, the first iron lid by the kitchen door lifted and floated off then one in a rose bed lower down, over flowed washing the soil down the road side and a hundred yards on the into a road drain. It was very fortunate that it was all done with clean cold water. The system passed its test but its capacity was a little suspect, and for a while the header tanks seemed to be under sized and took a while for the water pressure to recover. A fire hose on the top floor seemed to be in vacuum (negative pressure) so it was a good job no one suggested testing the fire drills at the same time.

On the middle floor lived the bursar, and at night he would go on patrol at a predicted time. It was timed soon after one such patrol, that two of us were to go down to the battery hen house, just down the college road to collect a dozen eggs for late night supper. Then quietly into the small room (one was on each floor) where there was a kettle and a toaster for the students use, when on early call for milking or stock duties. All the eggs were quietly put into the electric kettle, filled with water and switched on, four slices of bread were put in the toaster ready to switch on when a bursar alarm was heard (his door opening). All six of our group went hell for leather back into bed was fast asleep in seconds, after half hour of prowling about the bursar settled and his door shut again.

Gingerly but very quickly we went to rescue the eggs, it was too late, the kettle had boiled dry, the egg shells had turned black but very hard boiled. The kettles did not turn themselves off at that time and the small amount of water in with the eggs soon disappeared, so the kettle, burnt out, was spirited into the dust bins by the main kitchens, and a fresh one acquired from the store room adjacent to the dining room.

The leader of our group at Rodbaston (there was six groups of six lads and two groups of six of girls) clashed with a lad in another group, so much that one day one ended up being thrown into the pool in the garden and horticulture section, I would call it a pit with dirty black mud in the bottom. The pool was full of peat, or years of dead leaves, in my book I would call it a pit, but then it was landscaped and planted with shrubs, so now it's a lake. He was launched off the high bank head first into the pool, and came out with weeds round his shoulders and thick black mud from head to toe. The second big clash came a few weeks later when the victimized victim had his hair cut off in lumps and steps right down to his skull. He never canted or complained to anyone in authority, but it was plain to see his haircut was involuntary. On his weekend off he must have gone home and his parents; they were not impressed and reported their complaint to the top man the principle. There was a full enquiry into the incident which ended up with the aggressor being expelled.

After that it left me as leader of a short group only five for the next two terms, all the practical work had been calculated to six in the groups so we had on occasions to work all the harder.

In the rotation of practical training we undertook, one was horticulture, and to get about the Halls extensive gardens a group of students and all the tools, they had a three wheel motorized tipping cart. The single front wheel was the same size as a tractor rear wheel, and in the hub of the wheel was a single cylinder Petter engine. The frame of the cart came up from under the body in a goose neck onto a king pin on top of the front wheel, the driver stood inside the goose neck at the controls and it had a vertical steering wheel. It was designed to carry one ton, and at one time used by the county council highways department, who had any number of such vehicles. When they were made redundant in that department one was assigned to Rodbaston Horticultural department.

The head of that department was driving us briskly alongside the walled garden in the three wheeled cart, and being a little unstable he had to concentrate hard on keeping on the narrow track. On the back we all five of us were making it sway about, until we came to the corner, then we all threw ourselves onto the wrong side of the cart. This had a dramatic impact on its stability; it tipped us all out into a huge rhubarb patch (a soft landing) the driver as well. No one was hurt, but our man in charge never knew that we were really to blame for the up tip; he hurriedly got us to right the cart and asked us not to report the incident. With the clumsy driver being head of department, that cart was decommissioned shortly afterwards as too unstable for the job.

Same story but this time in verse

To Farming College I Was Sent

When I was in my late teens,
farming college I was sent,
To learn the latest way of doing
thing, but it only meant,
Living away from home all
week, at times weekends anall,
First time slept away from home,
in a hard bed by the wall.

No where else to sleep,
but in this old and worn bedstead,
Its springs were slack and hung,
like a hammock not a bed,
The mattress was so thin,
had an imprint on its back,
Of diamond pattern bed
springs, like sleeping on a rack.

It had iron bed posts one each
corner, tilted to the middle,
Only narrow like a ladder,
would make good tater riddle,
A couple of sleepless nights at first,
then slept like a log,
Getting out next morning,
it was a blooming slog.

Eight o'clock the breakfast bell,
half an hour for that,
Plenty of eggs and bacon,
cornflakes or porridge splat,
Tutors at the top table,
in a row they sat,
Students were in groups of
six, very quietly they chat.

Eight groups of six there was,
time table of duties given,
Alternate weeks it was early start,
to the livestock bidden,
A group for milking and a group
for pigs to feed and clean,
Group for sheep and poultry,
five thirty start not keen.

The next week it spoiled you,
lay in till breakfast bell,
Lectures every morning,
from nine to lunch time I do tell,

Afternoons back to the farm,
maintenance chore to do,
And the afternoon stock duties,
till five pm and that'll do.

College was having trouble
with the big house drains,
Rodding flushing all the rest,
a hose pipe from the mains,
So word went round students,
thought we could give a hand,
A bigger flush was what they
wanted, so together we band.

It was decided what we do,
store up water for very big flush,
Ten big deep baths on three floors,
filled and kept it hush,
Fourteen wash basins also filled,
waited for the bell to go,
All the plugs were pulled at once,
every toilet flushed also.

This surge of water lifted lids,
all the way the pipe did wend,
Flooded flower beds down the
drive, happened at weekend,
It cleared the drain of silt
and ***, no more faffing about,
Enquiry held, but it did the job,
to no one they could shout.

Was curfew each night at ten,
hunger pains start to show,
I wasn't alone that same night,
and we felt a bit gung-ho,
Boiled eggs we thought,
with fresh bread and butter,
Fetched dozen from battery hens,
all whispering in a mutter.

Tiptoed past the bursars door,
for he was a light sleeper,
Got the eggs back to boil,
landing kitchen kettle no cooker,
Got dozen eggs in electric kettle,
filled to brim with water,
Then it had just got to boil,
bursar was seen by our spotter.

All back to bed, good half hour
afore his door closed,
Crept round to the landing
kitchen, a smoking kettle nosed,
Eggs boiled hard black and
burned, water boiled and gone,
Kettle started to melt, no auto
switch to switch off and on.

Ruined our night and ruined
our kettle, no early cuppa for us,
Binned the kettle n eggs welded in,
cold morning drink we cus,
In a couple of days another
old kettle we found,
Didna try that again, electric main,
in all cost us two pound.

Learned how to cut hedges,
brushing hook down wards strokes,
Get the hedge to an 'A ' shape,
hawthorn had good hopes,
Principle cut his garden hedge,
to demonstrate how to do,
This skill and method short-lived,
machines invented anew.

Learned to shear the sheep,
New Zealand method by gum,
Clear the belly up the throat,
down the shoulder and rump,
Pull the head up between ya knees,
shear the other side,
Release the head ewe will rise
and walk through ya legs astride.

Wrap the fleece all in one,
tail end n flanks to the middle,
Roll it tight cut ends outside,
with your knee bent double,
The neck you twist to form
a bon's, enough go round tuck in,
Pitch it into the woolsack,
tread it well down within.

On the pigs we helped farrowing,
piglets born by the dozen,
See they got under the lamp,
dry out and suck on a 'button'
In the first week they had,
and injection prevent anemia
Iron it was into their leg,
mid squeals made sure heard ya.

Cows were milked in stalls,
tied with a yolk to the neck,
Milk was recorded every day;
compare cows ration a check,
Ayrshire with quality milk,
good colour and butterfat too,
Calves reared as replacements',
suckle by the livestock crew.

Gardening n' horticulture also
learned, had no interest in that,
Pruning and preparing apple trees,
plums and pears we tat,
Seedlings in boxes out in cold
frames, harden off for a while,
Sit on hot pipes in the green house,
thaw out in case we got piles.

Sugar beet grown, all done by hand,
singling to pulling the root,
A harvester came to demonstrate,
the first one I'd seen to boot,
It broke down a time or two,
Modifications made a many,
But the work it saved, and backache
too, must be a pretty penny.

Dealers sent their latest tractor,
for students to try and admire,
When we get home old bangers,
persuade the old man retire,
So we could buy that new tractor,
diesel with starter and cab,
Spoils you when get back ,
old tractor remains on the tab.

Educations What You Want

Educations what you want,
or that is what I'm told,
Get on in life and see the world,
seek your pot of gold.
More to life than toil and sweat,
let others soil their hands,
Let education guide the way, 9 till 5,
five day week demand.

Over the years most folk done this,
for better jobs travelled,
Men they left the land in droves,
off into town they pedaled.
With better money bought a car,
get about much quicker,
Then travelled even further
a field, became the city slicker.

———————-

Education is what survives when what has been learned has been forgotten
  B F Skinner (1904-1990)

Chapter 19

Norfolk Four Coarse Rotation (1950's at College)

All the young farm college students will laugh me off this page, because there does not seem to be such a thing as a full rotation these days. It seems a rotation for pests and diseases, and that's all. What you young un's must understand that there is a rotation to cope with weeds, mostly annual weeds.

These are what build up in arable land into a "seed bank" this needs a break and a rest for a few years in grass. We were learned the basic rotation devised by "Turnip Townshend" back in the 18th century, Roots, Barley, Seeds (two or three years), and Wheat.

Not all these old ideas can be rubbished off hand, and could well be adapted to suit the modern farming methods. You need to assess how much nitrogen can be "fixed" by a good two year stand of predominantly a red clover/grass mix, clover left to mature and flower into a tall crop of hay/silage, has a tremendous root system with the accompanying nitrogen fixing nodules, bigger the top growth the bigger the roots.

In years gone by there was no bagged fertilizer, and this method improved output and yield, only now a tittle of nitrogen on top of the above idea could well would match many of the modern yields of today. The moral of this story is to cut costs, i.e. nitrogen and not plant second wheat's. Now oilseed rape will cover as a root crop in this rotation, and to those who have never heard of it, under sow the barley with the grass / clover mixture. Time the seeding right and a bit of good fortune with the weather, and you soon get the hang of a good rotation saving on sprays as well

Norfolk Four Course Rotation (1950's at college)

At farming college we were told,
important it was to learn,
The basic four coarse rotation,
good yields a living to earn,
Roots Barley Seeds Wheat,
it kept the ground in good heart,
This was the basic rotation,
from which to make a good start.

Roots you hoed around until,
the leaves met in the row,
Smother any smaller weeds,
nowhere for them to grow,

Always left a good clean field,
and always in good heart,
Next crop had the benefit,
of getting a jolly good start.

Spring barley follows roots, too
strong a land it will soon go flat,
Drilled in March when soil is
warms, even plant stand begat,
Under sown with grass and red
clover, establishing the best
Docks were pulled and thistles
'spudded', first crop for to harvest.

Seeds grow on, once barley's off,
sheep graze in back end,
It tillers and bulks tremendously,
for winter feed depend,
Red clover with its vigorous
growth, roots beneath to match,
Fixes fertility down in the soil,
side to side of the patch.

Graze the seeds and keep it low,
doesn't produce the roots,
Fertility from sun to leaves,
small leaves stems and shoots,
Mown for hay grown to maturity,
for two years if you can,
Give you a wheat crop you never
had, at least that's the plan.

When the hays been cleared,
and fresh good cover of green,
Plough it in, green manure,
the clover roots have been,

Fix Nitrogen in the nodules,
best crop of wheat you've seen,
No sprays or artificial needed,
to return to a proper rotation I'm keen.

Organically done, this is the way,
make the sun and leaves,
Draw the goodness naturally;
a shower of rain receives,
Plants working how they ought
to, complement each other,
A good plant stand, and big broad
leaves, weeds you hope to smother.

I was fortunate in that my father helped me set up on my own 96 acre rented farm, and helped in that I could "borrow" odd thing and machinery from time to time. I started with 26 milking cows, and he let me make my own mistakes, as he said you learn quicker that way, particularly if it hits you in the pocket. But I have known a lot who have worked for or with their fathers, and have had to wait years before they are allowed to take the "reigns"

It's a Fifty Year Apprenticeship

The farmers still a learner,
till his eyes begin to blear,
Apprenticeship under the old man,
for at least fifty years,
Ruled in turn by his father,
the old ways are always best,
What bit of money he ever made,
in land he must invest.

From round the kitchen table,
the orders given out,
What to grow and sell and buy,
and what to do without,
Frugel's what you call it,
but he always has last say,
All his life, make do and mend,
only time for work, no play.

Seventy five is just about when;
he says he's had enough,
Say to the young ones now,
in their fifties, now it's tough,
Modernize and hit the cheque book,
let's get up to date,
First time after all these years,
they say it's never too late.

Old ideas and old ways have a habit of being re-invented, so try to keep some old ideas in the back of your mind, they may come in handy someday.

Ideas have to be planted, before they can come into fruition.

The definition of a weed --- **A weed is just a plant out of place.**

Chapter 20

I Knew the Old Gypsy was about to "Skin Me"

I knew the old gypsy was about to "skin me" with what he wanted for the horse, and gradually got round to a price three times what I had in mind.
The only horse to ever to pull it cart north bound on the M6.

Boswell the old Gypsy

It was around 1975 when we heard that Boswell the old gypsy who lived on his own permanent site just outside Stafford wanted to sell his horse. He was getting too old and infirm to work collecting scrap iron, as he had done round our area for years, he had got two daughters who used to work with him at times and knew the job. But they "modernized" and got a transit van, and found they did not have to work out in all weathers, and they seemed to be more the "rag and bone man" type of gypsies.

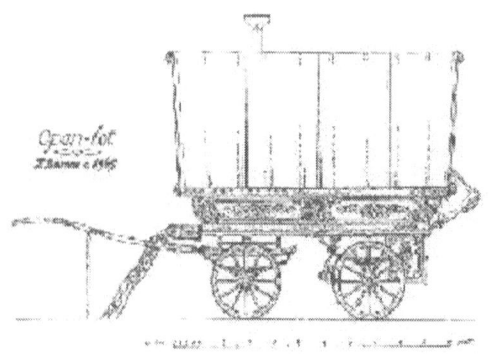

So I called to see him in his old bow top wagon, where he had slept underneath it all his life, and his misses and the children had slept inside.

He was inside with his little cast iron stove going and a pipe in his mouth, Being the bloke he was, I knew he was about to "skin me" with what he wanted for the horse, and gradually got round to a price three times what I had in mind. We walked across some rough ground towards where the horses were tethered, each one staked down to its own circle. The one we walked to, was a half legged honey coloured Dunn with beautiful dark main and tail and dark lower half to her legs and feathers. She was tethered to a shiny chain, the chain was directly round her neck with a nut and bolt through the links, the reason for this I discovered much later when we tried to tie her up by a stable. She did not like being tied short to a wall of fence, and she would pull backwards till the rope was tight and the lift her head with a snatch and break whatever was the weakest be it the fence, the ring on the wall, the rope or more usually it was the head collar.

Back to Boswell, he stuck and stuck on his price till I asked him to throw in the little four wheeled flat wagon and the harness, and he would have a deal. I won't divulge how much he charged, but he seemed pleased, and the cash was duly paid, and the horse "Dolly" was walked home.

Dolly enjoyed the freedom of being loose for the first time in her life, in a small paddock close to the house; she was eventually mixed with a couple more ponies who she dominated beyond belief. It was okay through the grazing season, but when hay or a bit of corn was brought into the field she was first in there, she would stand over the food and even we dare not go near her, turning her backside round to you and threatening with her heals. She could be caught all right with a bit of corn in the bucket and keep hold of the bucket while slipping a head collar on and she led okay.

Our daughters soon got a saddle on her and a bridle that had no blinkers, this she was not used to, and she soon got used to the idea of being under the saddle. One slight problem when walking her on the roads, particularly narrow country lanes, was that she insisted on walking four foot away from the kerb or the hedge bank. This she had done all her working life pulling the gypsy's dray, and no matter how much the girls pulled on the left reign, all she did was turn her head round to the side and keep walking four foot from the side of the road. She never lost that habit all the while we had her.

When Boswell had her they trotted off as far as ten miles out from his camp, on the search for scrap iron. On this one occasion he was out at Penkridge, and had set off back home when he realized that the M6 had just opened a few days before. Not being able to read or write, he could not read the big signs, so proceeded to trot Dolly up the slip road of junction 13, his camp was half a mile off junction 14 so this was a good short cut for him and his horse and cart.
At this point I must say that it was only the short five mile section between 13 & 14 that was opened, by the then minister of transport just a few weeks before. They had trotted along the hard shoulder and had got about half way when they were stopped by the police; all they could do was escort them the remaining way to J14 and home. This incident was reported on all the television news stations that night and in the new papers the following day as well. Dolly was the first and only horse to use the M6 motorway. By today's standards it was very quiet only local traffic using it and also at that time there was no upper speed limit, and it attracted all the "boy racers"

In time I acquired an old float, one that had been used to take milk churns to the station and pigs to market, not anything flash. It had at some point in time had its wooden wheels replaced with blow up rubber tyres, it had still got its original springs which made it a very comfortable ride. Our girls would be 12 and 14 years old and they used to take Dolly out with the float, the only seat was a broad plank wood, then had the long leather reigns through a guide on the front board of the float. They only walked her, but were often gone two or more hours at a time, the one time when they got home they were most excited about two daffodils they had picked. "You will never guess where these are from" and we did not guess. It turned out that they had travelled about six or seven mile round trip through Ranton, a neighbouring village, and just outside this village lived the "Black Sabbath" or most likely the lead member of that group, no other than Ozzy Osborne and his wife Sharron Osborne, and the little kids Jack and his sister. The girls were big fans of Black Sabbath and played their records at home very loud.

It turned out that while they were spying on the house they decided to take home a souvenir, the two daffodils. Before they could set off home again, with the excitement they had to have a wee, and where better to have a wee than through a hole in the bottom of this old float.

While I'm name dropping we used to have Chris Tarrant come to our local pub, and Lord Litchfield I remember got refused entry to the Holly Bush one night because he was wearing jean's, the land lord did not recognize him, and would not let him in. They had a strict dress code to keep out the "ruffians".

However back to Dolly, this is the same story in verse, which I had written some while ago

I Remember Old Dolly The Gypsy Horse

We bought a horse her name was Dolly,
a half legged mare was she,
A honey light coloured Dun,
black mane n tail black
feathers to the knee,
She had big feet and took big shoes,
over six inches and more across,
And walk with feet dead in line,
deliberate strides as if I'm the boss.

Bought her off a gypsy,
the Boswells from by Stafford Common,
There they had a bow top van,
they had a permanent site for one,
Grazing enough for three horses,
and a flat four wheel dray,
This they collected scrap iron,
from far and wide they stray.

It was a day when he took old Dolly,
with the four wheel dray,
All the way to Penkridge,
collecting scrap along the way,
On the way back he noticed
that the new motorway just opened,
So along the hard shoulder he trundled,
him his journey shortened.

This horse it had a mind all its own,
would not share its hay,
Stood in the middle of the pile,
teeth and heels would kick away,
Every one and everything,
defend it to the death,
No wonder she looked so big
savored and healthy, every breath.

First time we put on a saddle, s
he had no blinkers not perturb,
Walking down the road she walked,
two paces from the kerb,
This was all of her experience,
of pulling in the shaft,
No pulling on the reigns would make
her change her way of graft.

———————-

**For the want of a nail,
the shoe was lost,
for the want of a shoe
the horse was lost,
and for the want of a horse
the rider was lost,
being overtaken and
slain by the enemy,
all for the want of care
about a horse shoe nail.**

Benjamin Franklin (1706-1790)

Chapter 21

Need Long Toe Nails Like Claws to Grip on the Perch

Dad always said that,
"You're only as good as your feet,"
But then he was talking bout,
horse's cows and bullocks for meat.

Anyone who died in the village were said to have "Fell off the perch"

Yes this is a picture of a picture, and my place is the farm top left with the eight bay hay barn, top in the middle on the same side of the road is the pub, and middle on the left is the village school, they have over two hundred kids from all the villages around and some come from out of town. Right of middle is St Chads church and guess who lives under the star (The Vicar in the vicarage.) There used to be four farms and four herds of cows in this area of the village but mine is the last one to survive, when I give up my tenancy even that will go as well.

As Old as what you Feel

They always say that you're only,
as old as what you feel,
Now I like to have knap,
after almost every meal,
And in the night get disturbed,
got to water me hoss,
So now I think I must be old,
me legs I cannot cross.

The old body that I've worked with,
all my living years,
Getting tired and old as well,
confirming all my fears,
Joints get stiff and muscles ache,
cannot move so fast,
Stumble over rough ground,
getting all harassed.

I cannot read the paper,
until my glasses I must find,
Remember where I put them,
must be getting blind,
The misses she has got them on,
cannot find her own,
Each of us both as bad,
but then we shouldn't moan.

Feet I cannot reach right now,
back won't bend so much,
Got to have chiropodist,
corns and toe nails to retouch,

Dad always said that,
you're only as good as your feet,
But then he was talking bout,
horse's cows and bullocks for meat.

Hair it has all gone grey,
and very thin on top,
Need a hat in winter,
the freezing cold wind to stop,
No insulation gainst the cold,
a wig I got in mind,
But then its two lots of hair to
comb, as well as going blind.

Ya mind is getting slower,
reactions far too late,
The young ones like to drive,
my driving they berate,
A dent or two I don't mind,
but it frightens them to death,
When they're sitting in the back
and cannot catch their breath.

So now I try to look relaxed,
put me feet up on me chair,
Central heating turned up,
find me glasses and combed me hair,
Slippers on oh what bliss,
the telly's far too loud,
Lost the bloody controller now,
good job were not too proud.

It funny how your mind can wander when you're thinking of nothing in particular, thinking about mothers old soft water tank outside the back door and the sock come filter tied round the tap to filter out the house sparrow droppings, and how she used to wash our hair in it because it lathered better, all this when we were kids, The different colored bottles that medicine came in up on the top shelf, very few if any tablets as I can remember. The only "tablet" I can remember was disguised as dark chocolate, and after we had each had a square of it, were told it was for worms. I can remember the strong taste of it now, and it put me off chocolate for life. The wobbly stool, the dragging wicket, and the postman with no nose, he had had a close encounter with a bullet or shrapnel in the war and lost his nose, there was just two holes in his face between his eyes, and he cycled eight to ten miles out and back to the village six days a week. A very brave and respected man for his courage working as a postman in all weathers.

Now we've Got a Leaking Tank

Now we've got a leaking tank,
soft water leaking out,
Got to find a bung for it,
a cork or something stout,
A cork from in a bottle,
would do the job okay,
Bottles in the cupboard,
we've got a good array.

Tall bottles short bottles,
white or blue or green,
Embrocation medication,
colour codes it seems,
For coughs and colds a
spoon full, taken every day,
Bumps and bruises rub it on,
oily vapors say.

Way back on the top shelf,
   most of them half used,
Find a chair to stand on,
   now I'm all confused.
Old chair it's wobbly,
   one leg is short and loose,
Take it in the workshop;
   it's had some abuse.

Other three cut them off,
   make legs same length,
On the leg bit of glue,
   stick it to give it strength,
But the saw it's lost some teeth,
   and it wouldn't cut,
Gate into the back yard,
   and that it wouldn't shut.

Timber on it rotten and
   hinge it would not hold,
Aught to have a new one
   or that is what I'm told,
Keep out intruders,
   this it wouldn't do,
Post that it hangs on,
   that also must renew.

There's another sort of post,
   which goes in a letter box,
Brought by the postman,
   from his bike he always locks,
Parcel to deliver, on the
   door he always knocks,
On his round six days a week,
   wearing out his socks.

It was always an old sock,
which was tied around the tap,
This it filtered all the water,
floating bits to trap,
On the front of this old tank,
I think I've found a cork,
Stop the water leaking,
out faster than it aught.

They always said that,
You're once an adult and twice a child in life.

When Gravity Takes Over

It is not until people
of your own age,
Start falling off perch
begin to engage,
Your mind to thinking
what you will do,
When you're the last one
at hundred and two,

Gravity takes hold and
pulls everything down,
From your cheeks on
your bottom to facial frown,
Everything sags and
get a lot shorter,
When you get into that
last century quarter.

Memory is one thing that
you take for granted,
Forgetting to remember
is not to be vaunted,
They say it's selective in
what you do,
It's a privilege to have choice
than get in a stew.

Toe nails can't reach and
look like bald eagle,
Chiropodist trims and tells
you they're fungal,
Gives you some cream and
still you can't reach,
Old back bone won't bend
but still got my speech.

The hair it still grows
with the utmost vigor,
Round wrinkly face and
chin it gets bigger,
Stretch and contort to
shave it all off,
But some it gets missed
when got a bad cough.

As you wobble out to
the car that you drive,
Dented on the corners,
too bad to describe,
Backing is dangerous
blind as a bat,
Makes not much difference
just one more splat.

To round up and sum up
the older you get,
Experience all round but
you do forget,
Long toe nail like claws
to grip onto the perch,
Live on forever not left in the lurch.

The human race has one really effective weapon; laughter

Chapter 22

The Great escape "Getting out of Me Chair"

I was stranded. The misses was out of earshot, and it was too dangerous for her to wander about in the dark and come down stairs.

Well it happened, it was going to happen sometime, and it happen the other night, and we had a power cut. Sitting comfortable as you do in the evening watching TV, we had just had a cup of tea at supper time and the misses had gone up to bed, I was half an hour behind her but just before my program had finished the electric went off.

As you may know the family bought me a new chair for my 70th and I was well flat out on it, feet well up and head up just enough to see the TV, and as I said the chair is operated from the plug on electric, so I was stranded. The misses was out of earshot and was too dangerous for her to wander about in the dark and come down stairs as well, so as described in my thoughts about this situation where I warned myself about a power cut. Having sat for five minutes thinking it might come on again shortly, it did not happen, so like a tortoise on its back.

It's a recliner chair, the back goes down almost flat and it lifts ya feet up level and its operated with an electric controller off the mains. I started swinging my legs up in the air and eventually managed to roll out of the chair over the arm rest, landing on my "tin" knees on all four in the middle of the carpet. This was the safest way to move about to the door when I clawed my way up the door post, felt my way along the hallway to the office where I knew where I had got a windup modern torch. All this took best part of fifteen minutes and went up to check her indoors was Okay.

We both sat in the dark on the bed discussing the programs we had respectively been watching and sat laughing about my "great escape". However the power was restored after about an hour and half and I went down to "drive" my chair back into its parking position, ready for my next knap after lunch tomorrow.

On reflection if I had been patient I could have stayed in the chair until it came back on, but at that time of night I also have the need to "water me hoss" so I demonstrated to myself how agile I was, and just wonder how it will pan out in say twenty years' time when I'm "OLD".

Life's Time Clock You Cannot Beat

You wonder where the time,
and all the years have gone,
They pass so quickly now,
going one by one,
Season's sequence come in turn,
no control have we,
Wind and rain and sunshine,
day and night decree.

Snow and frost in winter,
good start for New Year,
Spring and summer showers,
and the sun appear,
Autumn fruits and berries,
winter for the birds to eat,
Repeat with little change,
life's time clock cannot beat.

The best way to escape from a problem is to solve it.
Alan Saporta

Chapter 23

Climate Change the Hot Topic
(Or cold depending what year it was)

I recall the winter of 1947 when we had a lot of deep snow which filled the roads and lanes level full to the top of the hedges in places as deep as ten foot. There was a continuous period of cold weather that the snow hung about for all of a month, and frost most nights freezing the water bowls in from of the cows tied in their stalls. The cows were loosed out each day for a couple of hours for exercise and if they had no water in the shed, we had to break the ice on the flowing brook. Nowadays we do get a bit of snow and often melted away by mid-morning

That's me on the right in 1947, when the roads were blocked for almost a week. In places the road was filled up to the top of the hedges eight or ten feet, almost walk on top of the fences and hedges.

Picture was taken with the Beeches Farm in the back ground, and the original old beech trees. The tall chap with the leather jerkin was a bus driver, John Lowe, and the chap with his ass in the air was a cow man from Village Farm named George. My mum is the one in the light coloured coat at the back. On the left is John's daughter Margaret, and in the middle is George's daughter Kath.

I Remember Digging Snow 1947

I Remember digging snow,
with my little spade,
I would be about eight years old,
my friends and me we played
Little caps and scarves we wore,
And wellington boots as well,
Digging under snow drifts,
till roof top down it fell.

All the men from in the village,
started to dig the road,
Drifts for over a mile each way,
they all toiled and strove,
To get the hay from barn to shed,
out lying cattle to feed,
Even the tractors couldn't move,
or get to hog of swede

The village it was totally cut off,
for about two days,
Us kids we dug up to houses,
digging out the pathways
For this we got a piece,
of home made cake with jam,
Or a drink of Corona pop,
just a little dram.

Bread man was the first,
to venture in on foot,
Helped along the way,
on our sledges bread he put,

The postman he was helped,
slippery paths we ran up,
Paper lady old Violet,
her papers did not turn-up.

Milk from the farms still there,
to double in two days,
Take to Bridgeford Garage,
across the fields on drays,
Bring back the empty churns,
all clanging on the back,
To fill again them over night,
and back along same track.

Third day we went to school,
Miss Pye from Doxey walked, (our
teacher)Only six of us turned up,
on board in front of fire she chalked,
Chairs and a table pulled to the fire,
roaring up the chimney,
Compared our notes about,
through snow we had to journey.

When the snow ventualy melted,
lumps of drifts stayed put,
It took weeks for this to go,
from under hedge and butt,
Floods came out all over low ground,
silt and mud abound,
Pleased when the spring came along,
thought the grass had drowned.

After mains water came to the village in the 1950's I remember one very hard frost that went on for a week and it froze the mains water pipes which supposed to be three foot down. The week after water still would not run and they brought in a man with a big welding generator, and connected his live cable to one fire hydrant, and run a long cable to connect his earth to the next hydrant, and run a currant though the pipes for about twenty minutes or until the water run. It took him all day to do the half mile length of the village. There had been a covering of snow off the road line and that seemed to prevent most house pipes freezing to the house, but those that did the man connected his cable to the tap under the sinks.

In that same year when I remember the ford in the village had frozen over that solid that it carried the tractor and trailer, for a two day muck carting spree without breaking through. When it did break in the middle the tractor dropped about eighteen inches and had a job to get it out, then could not use that route for a few weeks due to the deep steps down off the ice at the sides.

In the 1970's (think it was 75 or 76) we had that very dry hot summer that burned off all the grass and I resorted to grazing my cows down the cow lane which is almost a mile long and stayed with then for an hour each morning for them to eat off the hedge banks and lane verges, then taking them onto the peaty meadows where the fields were green no grass but just green and down there for water. The wheat and barley had quite good heads considering but the straw was about six inches high, the combine was licking it off the ground. No straw to bale on most of the fields.

The Millian Brook that flows through the ford stopped flowing for the first time in living memory, there were still deep pools of water along its length but the different herds of cattle drank more than what came from the springs that fed it.

Church Farm is just up the lane off the picture to the right, this is the ford and the foot bridge where most of the cows would prefer to queue up and go over single file, although odd one would always go through even when it was in flood and almost four foot deep. When it froze over it was around two foot deep, some water would find its way over the top and freeze again at night giving and ever stronger icepack.

The Millian Brook

The Millian Brook from fields filtrate,
All the water from the Seighford estate,
Same steady contour for years gone by,
    Nothing to stop it, even if you try.
    Through pools and weirs all man made,
        It burst its bank its time outstayed
    Through drought and flood to the ford
    Its waters gouge its path contoured.

It winds its way through fields and meadows,
Under dark shade beneath the willows,
Between the alders hold banks well rooted,
    Foot bridge now once it was waded.

The brook alive with wildlife so shy,
Wade and nest and burrow rely,
From flies and fish to mammals and birds,
All can be found as it wends seawards.

Advice is like snow; the softer it falls, the longer it dwells upon, and deeper it sinks into the mind.
Samuel Taylor Coleridge (1772-1834)

Chapter 24

Exploring the Bacon Pits (1948)

It was always depressing, the thought of having to go back to school after an exciting weekend exploring up on the old airfield that had just closed. We were sent out from home in good time, to walk the half mile up the village to school, but we met up with our mates on the way and walked even slower, more often than not the bell had gone just before we had arrived.

This is the village school, the main block and the entrance is on the left, the School House on the right hand side with its own front door.

They had just started school dinners, for which mother sent us with one shilling and a penny for five dinners, (that just over 5p in new money for the week). No choice you just had eat what was sent on the van or do without. On the whole we seemed to eat most things, and those that refused, meant that we could have as "seconds", and an almighty clamor to get to the front of the queue for that. In certain class rooms you could see the church clock and could not wait for three thirty and home time.

First day of the week to school

Monday morning what a drag,
five whole days of school,
Get up slowly rubbing eyes,
washed ourselves in water cool,
Down for breakfast a glass
of milk ,porridge in a bowl,
Tie our shoes and jacket on,
out the door we strolled.

Up the village join our mates,
dawdled all the way,
School bell it had just gone,
what a long old day,
Strode through the gates,
my brothers our mates and me,
See what mood the teacher's in,
try to educate you see.

Take the register, next assembly,
then chant times tables all,
English history geography,
and learn all about Nepal,
We learned about the plants
and trees, gardening as well,
Germinate a bean in jar,
see its roots and shoots all swell.

Good to hear the final bell,
home we race full speed,
There to see what mother baked,
just to fill our need,

Change of clothes and out to play,
often have some jobs,
Feed the hens and collect the eggs,
all with fresh baked cobs.

In 1944 to 1950, when I was there, there was a very old lady lived in the school house with her daughter, the daughter worked in town, and the mother was often left in bed at home on her own. Her bedroom window over looked the playground. No one was allowed to play in that area for fear of disturbing her, but she almost caught us this one day when she opened the window and emptied the contents of the pee pot just missing us, she was shouting at all the kids got and we bit excited as to what would have happened if it had landed on us.

It was around the time the airfield closed in 1948, and I would be 10 years old we found a way to get up onto the perimeter track of the old war time aerodrome. The bomb dumps around the woods that surrounded the airfield still had the full fake grass camouflage netting over. We explored all round them inside and out, to see if any bombs had been left behind. There must have been ten or more of these dumps all-round the outside of the perimeter track tucked under the sides of different woods. One wood that intrigued us was "Williams" wood, and we had heard the old men of the village taking about two pits in the middle of this wood that were called the "Bacon Pits".

The gates were still closed and the airfield was patrolled by a guard to stop just such kids as us. So we were very frightened going in and even more frightened on the way out of the wood, so much so that with short trousers and brambles and nettles, we never felt them until we had a count up to see if we were all there, then there was evidence of blood, and scratches from coming out in such a rush.

I Remember Exploring the Bacon Pits.

We went to Seighford Airfield,
soon after it had closed,
To have a look for William's wood,
and find the mystery posed,
We heard tales about the pits,
in middle of the wood,
These were called The Bacon Pits,
and thought we would explore.

On our bikes we did set out,
along the perimeter track,
Turned off through the bomb dumps,
into the far outback,
We came along the side the wood,
and down we dropped our bikes,
Decided to go through the under growth,
must be a big long hike.

Our legs were scratched and nettled,
but soldier on we must,
Our nervous tension it was showing,
the guard we might be cussed,
Out in an opening, first pit we could see,
deep in the wood through the leaves,
The pool was dark, the water smooth,
surrounded by tall trees.

We found a stick for each of us,
to beat the brambles down,
A path to make so we could find,
the pools of such renown,

Eerie echo's thought we heard,
while progress it was bumbling,
Looking up for what we could hear,
the sticks the scrub a thwacking.

Press on to find the second pool,
onwards through the scrub to find,
Each step we took cracked the twigs,
not knowing whose behind
It was difficult to keep on moving,
eventually we found it,
We all stood still and thought that we
could, hear the enemy emit.

Thinking that we were being chased,
an almighty scramble started,
Following the path came in,
and round first pit we darted,
A mate behind through in a stone,
and frightened us the more,
Shouting squealing cracking of twigs,
went even faster, such uproar.

Having got back to our bikes,
we had a count to see,
If all the men had got back,
none drowned or captured by a Nazi,
We peddled fast all scratched and bleeding,
home to safety to our mums,
Blood wiped off all patched and plastered,
then had a meeting all us chums.

———————

**What about this then, it's so modern,
It's plastic.**

Plastic Card

Down to do the shopping,
they're open till very late,
Paid for on a plastic card,
flexible friend a mate,
A number that they call a pin,
must be punched in right,
This can use any time,
even day or night,
Slong as money's in the bank,
it will spit it out,
Over drawn is evil,
of money you've got a drought.
Spending more than what
you've got, do ya sums all wrong,
The trouble that it causes,
bank letters they are long,
Makes ya sweat and worry,
and cannot settle down,
Pace about and have a shout,
it gives ya face a frown.

Earth and sky, woods and fields, lakes and rivers, the mountains and the sea, are excellent school masters, and teach some of us more than we can ever learn from books *John Lubbock (1834-1913*

Chapter 25

Mother Always Worked So Hard

Back in the 1950's there were six of us to sit round the kitchen table for meal times, plus for a few years dads brother, Uncle Jack, that made seven. It was around this time that mother had to have some help in the house each morning for about three hours. It was not like we were away at work all day, we were all in for every mealtime and no letup. For quite a while we came home from school at lunch time, before the days of school dinners.

Mother Always Worked So Hard   (1945)

Mother always worked so hard,
to rear her brood of kids,
As we grew bigger and in our teens,
we must have cost her quids,
Four of us lads and our dad,
Uncle Jack as well,
Looked after all of us,
knitting socks and jumpers she excelled.

Big appetites we had,
and thrifty she had to be,
Most things grown about the farm,
including all the poultry.
Eggs and chicken, more often
old hen, regular we had,
Potatoes beans and cabbage carrots,
all grown by our dad,

Rabbit pie most every week,
killed a pig and cured,
Only thing she did buy,
big lump of beef well matured.
Bottled all the fruit she could,
and salted down the beans,
Got the meals and baked the cakes,
did washing in between,

Baker came three times a week,
six loaves every call,
Corn flakes she also brought,
lot of boxes I recall,
Through the war and rationing,
never seemed go short,
Well fed, we all worked hard,
and not much time cavort.

At our peak before any of us left home the baker called three times a week and dropped of twenty loaves of bread The bread man took mothers grocery list on a Thursday and delivered the order on Saturday morning, this included five boxes of Kellogg's Cornflakes per week. There was no sliced bread in them days, and as we got older so the bread that mother got thicker and thicker slices.

The old thatched cottage up the road was the Woodman's Cottage

Woodman's Cottage

The Woodman he had a son and two daughters, and it was the middle daughter Dorothy who helped mother for getting on for twenty years, her brother Colin he worked as a fireman on the steam express trains

This is the woodman Arthur Lawson with Colin as a little lad and Dorothy standing in front of him also their dog, the younger daughter Audrey would be younger still. This picture would be around 1930.

This old house was taken down when the new council houses were built in the village, and Dorothy got married she and her husband Bill moved into one and Arthur, her dad moved with them. The family lost their mother when they were still quite young.

I Remember Breakfast

I remember sitting down,
all six of us to breakfast, (7 including Jack)
Father always sat upon a bench,
he made it so it would last,
We all sat round with our chins,
ledged upon the table,
And watched as mother lifted out,
boiled eggs with a great big ladle,

The bread was hand sliced all in
doorsteps, a whole loaf at a time,
With scrape of butter,
and cut into fingers (not mine,)
Double yoked eggs we could
not sell, all boiled to a tee,
Salt and pepper for the oldest,
not including me.

Top chopped off the eggs we scoffed,
all waiting for our porridge,
A two gallon tub of best raw oats,
said to improve our knowledge,
The lid had tilted with the froth,
and glued it to the stove,
This had boiled two hours or more,
and into it we dove.
(No instant porridge them days)

The bowls were deep the spoons seemed small,
as mother dealt it out,
With fobs of stale bread in the bottom
there to fill us up no doubt,
Some had syrup some had sugar,
with milk the lot we floated,
But when this had gone, we had no space,
full to top and bloated.

When bacon breakfasts we did have,
cut from flitch in pantry,
Mother armed herself with carving knife,
the flitch hung from a gantry,
Twelve slices she would cut all thick,
no shrinking up or curling,
The lean and fat was of equal portions,
it didn't need much turning.

The doorstep bread as I have said
will float in fat from frying,
When turning black, it filled the kitchen,
with haze beyond denying,
It smelt good and tasted good,
with eggs, bacon, and black pudding,
This went down with mugs of tea,
the kettle was always boiling.

Out we went to work it off,
all satisfied and jolly,
Come hail or rain or sunshine,
we always knew that we,
Were waterproofed from inside,
top of head to feet,
With mother's special breakfast,
it kept in all the heat.

I Remember Mother taking us to Bed,
It was 1943 when there was only three of us.

When it came to seven o'clock,
and we all started yarning,
We had milk and Ovaltine,
nothing else till morning,

She carried us all up to bed ,
eldest on her back,
One each hip up the stairs,
enough make her crack.

Up the wooden hills we went,
she struggled to the top,
Flannel flashed around us,
and into bed we flopped,
First she made a great deep furrow,
deep in feather bed
Snuggled under, eiderdown
with worn out fluffy ted

Central heating not invented,
only one room warm,
Bedroom bove the kitchen,
the pillow fights were norm,
Father up the stairs he came,
in bed were we real quick,
Feathers floated round the bulb,
all snoring he would quip.

When father took his slipper off,
we knew he must be slow,
He chased us round the bedroom
and under bed we'd go,
Like rabbits down a bolt hole,
he couldn't get us out,
He never really hurt us, but he
had a dam good shout.

Don't be afraid of growing slowly, be afraid of standing still

Chapter 26

I Remember mother lighting the Kitchen fire

If the oven door was slightly open we found out that the cat even slept in the oven. But she soon found out that that was not a good place to be.

The kitchen range was the main source of heat for the whole house and it also had a back boiler to heat the water in the taps, so this was lit every morning of the year. Mother would put some chopped sticks on the hearth or in the bottom of the oven each night so the sticks would be dry as tinder for lighting the following morning. As you can imagine the hearth was a nice warm place for the cat to spend the night and if the oven door was slightly open we found out that the cat even slept in the oven. But she soon found out that that was not a good place to be.

A shovel full of ashes was cleared out from under the grate, some newspaper runkled up and sticks put on top then a shovel full of coal (best steam coal from the railway, rolled off a steam engine tender as it passed through our fields, dad knew the driver and they exchanged contraband when food was on ration). A match was applied and both dampers were pulled out to draw the fire round the oven and boiler, then she went on with other jobs such as getting breakfast for when morning milking had finished and we all came in.

Read on

I Remember Mother Lighting the Kitchen Fire

First job every morning,
is to light the kitchen fire,
It heats the water in the tap,
heat this end of house entire

Chopped sticks were placed,
hearth night before,
It catches light instantly,
and with damper out it roars.

One Sunday morning after breakfast,
when father tales us told,
We heard a scratching and a scowling,
from the oven wow behold,
Mother opened oven door,
out popped our poor old cat,
Door left part open night before,
to keep warm at that.

When mother put match to fire,
she latched the oven door,
To pre heat for Sunday joint,
not knowing who was indoors,
The poor hot cat shot out the door,
to cool off in the snow,
Not out there long the milk she sort,
she was all aglow.

Big shovel full of coal brought in,
and bank the fire up high,
The beef was put into the pan,
vast heat it was then to apply,
When part done and she looked in,
great waft of heat and haze,
Tatters placed around in fat ,
to roast till brown and brazed.

Our Sunday morning tales dad told,
lasted to coffee time,
As long as nothing else came up,
to delay the ending what a crime,

Then we all turned out, a brush apiece,
to sweep up round the yard,
All trying to imagine all the escapades,
round uncle Dan's farmyard.

Don't seem to have a relevant picture to this story so, this is just a picture of trees in our back fields, the big oak on the right is almost dead and is a prime candidate for firewood. (In fact it was cut down in autumn 2011)

Uncle Dan's Fire

This would have happened in the 1920's when father was in his teens; he and his mates were inquisitive as to know the sleeping arrangements of his uncle Dan and his house keeper. Them years ago straw was in battens not bales, so they decided that they needed to wake them up quickly in the middle of the night, and the best way was to light a fire in the middle of his front lawn, well lawn, it was a sheep grazed patch of grass round the house, lawn mowers for farmers were sheep. They brought a few battens of straw stood up wigwam stile and chucked in a match, when the fire had got going well, they stood round the corner and shouted FIRE.

Uncle Dan's Fire
I remember father telling us,
about his uncle Dan,
Lived in his farm house,
and they did get a plan,
His house keeper lived with him,
had to check which room,
And wondered how to find out,
they dare not assume.

They went round one night,
out to his front lawn,
Way after they had gone to bed,
curtains they were drawn,
Built a pile of straw there,
and set the lot alight,
Hiding round the corner,
twas middle of the night.

They had done all this,
and shouted loudly FIRE,
Only wanted to see witch window,
what was to transpire,
If they looked out same window,
that it would confirm,
What they suspected all along,
just to make him squirm.

Father never did tell us,
what the outcome was,
Told us we're too young,
to understand the cause,
Always looked after uncle Dan,
right up to the end,
Buried in Bradley church yard ,
his courage we commend.

It is with our passions, as it is with fire and water, they are good servants but bad masters.
Aesop (620 BC - 560 BC)

Chapter 27

The Cows Have Got a Leader and She Watches all the While

Miss her when she finally goes,
to meet her maker's bullet,
End up as tough as old leather boots,
n' fill a of pack of suet.

Well it's that time of year again (November) when the calves have got to be weaned, the shed has been prepare, the troughs along the front have got gates above them to stop the jumpers, the water trough has extra rails to stop them going through, enough bedding thrown down to last a month, a ring feeder positioned where it can be replenished from outside.

The cows will shout by their field gate for three days, and the fencing in that area checked, and a lane end gate kept shut as a long stop. Where the cows will be bellowing is at the bottom of the gardens of nine houses, all of whom are "city" types, so to try to keep them sweet I ring the end one up each year, to forewarn them of the impending noise.

The Suckler Cows

The suckler cows they graze all summer,
until we wean the calf,
When the calves we take away,
cows they bellow not by half,
The calves the same in shed we keep,
until they settle in,
Gates are high and fences too,
all to stop them from esca-apin.

Three days it lasts, until they feel,
the pain of hunger's stronger,
The cows they clear off down the field,
and hang about no longer,
Calves have no choice but stay,
feed them corn and feed them hay,
One month they need get used to living,
in the yard all in a bay.

They all get wormed and gain no weight,
till frettin they've forgotten,
Put them out on clean grass,
feed supplements, no silage rotten,
There they will grow and gain the weight,
they lost plus plenty more,
When at last they do get fat,
read the scales its there we can't ignore.

Below is Chocky a Simmental cross Friesian, leader of the herd, she is no oil painting but always has plenty of milk, you can see her long square face in the picture, how wide her muzzle is, almost as wide as her eyes. She is the one who has good eyesight and good hearing and always knows what is going on, on her patch.

One thing she cannot resist is a bucket with a bit of corn, and once she starts moving hopefully in the right direction the others tend to follow.

The Cows Have Got a Leader

The cows have got a leader,
and she watches all the while,
She knows exactly what ya doing,
sometimes make you smile,
Only got to touch the gate latch,
and up will go her head,
And walk towards the gateway,
without a word being said.

Go to count them every morning,
and check that they're all okay,
They think they want a new field,
and walk off all that way,
Oblige them at your peril,
as they mob you round the gate,
The fencings got to be strong,
if you've got to make them wait.

If more than one walks in the field,
leader walks the other way,
Takes the whole lot with her,
she must know its testing day,

Got to walk round whole dam field,
head them to the gate,
Seems that they have forgotten,
and vet's is here by eight.

Leader walking off right way,
the others following her lead,
Off towards the gateway,
but they're gathering speed,
All stop short of going through,
and start to circle round,
A young one makes a break for
freedom, loose the lot confound.

A bucket with a bit of corn,
the leaders up for that,
Always first one at the trough,
and give her a little pat,
She follows where you walking,
out off out down the lane,
Other think they're missing out,
and follow once again.

So cherish your old leader,
she can save you a lot of time,
Show the young cows where to go,
while she's in her prime,
Miss her when she finally goes,
to meet her maker's bullet,
End up as tough as old leather boots,
n' fill a of pack of suet.

Tongue- a variety of meat, rarely served because it clearly crosses the line between a cut of beef and a piece of dead cow   Bob Ekstrom, *Pitt, MN*

Chapter 28

Old characters Of the Village

Albert Hine
Describe the man were looking at,
a jerkin he did ware,
Tied round the middle with binder twine,
to hold more than just a tare,

These are many characters of the village all of whom worked about the farms, few if any traveled out to other parts for work. This is what I remember of Albert in the 1940's when I was a little lad.

Albert Hine was a hardworking man only short in stature, and quite round in his later years. He had a weather beaten face and small red veins showing on his chin and nose and red rims to his ears. More often than not he had a dark three or four day stubble on his chin. He always wore a cap as most men did at that time, on the few occasions that his hat was removed, or blown off, it revealed thinning flattened hair that had a permanent line where his cap fitted round his head, showing even more when he was sweating or when it was raining.
    He always wore a waist coat, an old jacket and a well-worn old leather jerkin. This was usually fastened round his middle with a piece of binder twine. On his feet were good stout hobnail boots that had been mended many times. Most men in the country areas all had their own lasts, and a box of hob nails. There was quite a few varieties of these nails, the single ones were nailed all-round the edge of the sole with triple nails spread around the centre of the sole. On the heel was a blacksmith made U-shaped tip and a smaller tip on the toe of his boots Round the calf of his legs he always had leggings which buttoned up the side of his leg and a small buckle at the

top to protect his corduroy trousers

On the club room night once or sometimes twice a week, the men of the village would meet for a game of snooker or games of dominoes and cards. On this occasion out would come his second best cap jacket and corduroy trousers (or put another way next year's work clothes).

The only other thing he wore (as opposed to carrying) was his pipe. This was not always lit, but when it was it was prodded full of tobacco with his fist finger that was permanently the same colour as the inside of his pipe. Out with his Swan Vesta`s (matches to those who don't know) match pinched between his thumb and first finger cupped with the lighted end in the palm to protect it from the wind and rain. Then he introduced it over the pipe, the flame now being drawn through the tobacco with intermittent clouds of smoke rising around his cap until it was well alight. This cupping of the hand was always the way it was done even at the Friday night whist-drives in the old club room, when there was no wind and rain.

Ivy Cottage, where Albert lived was one of a pair of farm cottages known as "Spite cottages", situated on the vicarage corner they were built to prevent the view from the Old vicarage to Seighford Hall half a mile away. (The vicar and the Lord of the Manor did not like each other and these cottages were put up to block the view from the vicarage hence the name "Spite Cottages") The other cottage is situated between it and St Chads Church.

As a tied cottage it belonged to the Yews Farm, and at one time it was occupied by the cowman, then latterly by Albert who was the wagoner. In the 1950's it was stripped of its ivy and both cottages were cement rendered and painted white.

This was Ivy Cottage where Albert lived (on the end of the Vicarage drive) and being only a short man he kept all his hedges quite short as well. Most of the garden was cultivated .Starting with the tallest items it was runner beans and as the row always seemed to run away from the road hedge, you could see the Church clock from anywhere along that part of the road. The next tallest thing was tobacco and as this was his largest crop area. When it came to maturity in September (it got to about three feet high) you could not see the clock.. This crop was cut in large leaves and hung to dry in the house to preserve them, then crisped up to rub into usable tobacco in the cool oven over night as and when required

Living next but one to St Chad's Church, he was a bell ringer, Thursday was the chosen night in the week was always kept as practice night, then every Sunday night between six and six thirty the bells were rung, then a few other special occasions like weddings or visiting ringers. In the belfry there was sometimes maintenance to be done, and if you look on the window sill of the south facing window you will find some cement that had been lettered with the names of all five ringers.

It was said in his younger days that he could walk out of the hills with a ewe under each arm such was the strength of this little man. As I said he lived at Ivy Cottage which was a farm cottage to Yews Farm where he worked as Wagoner for Charles Finnimore. You could not get a greater contrast of the sizes, between him being not a very tall man and the shire horses he worked with. When muck carting with a tipping cart that had five foot iron hooped wheels with one shire in the shafts and another in chains in front, he would walk along side with long plough lines (reigns) guiding the chain horse in front, travelling across the village green and up the Moss Lane to the fields belonging to the Yews.

He kept a couple of house cows of his own, and a few young stock on what is now the school playing field, and the small field adjoining at the end of Oldfords Lane (we call this field "Albert's Patch") . During the winter there is always water in a pool in between the two patches of ground, but in dry periods this dried up and he had to carry water from the Ford for the cattle.

By now (he had retired from employment but not from work) he had a little old tractor of his own with a carrying box on the back which held two forty gallon drums. A busy man, he mowed the church yard with a scythe. His principle reason was to turn it for a few days and make it into hay for winter fodder for his stock. He also cut the grass verges all the way to Doxey (over a mile) this was for the same reason. The hay he carted loose, as in the days before balers and stacked it in a tin roofed shed loose that he put up in one of the paddocks.

During the war, he like all the other men in the village were in the "Home Guard" (as in Dads Army) .He had to do training and be on duty on Rota, billeted in the wooden village hall at Great Bridgeford. On very cold nights the potbellied stove would be stoked up to the top with coke and glowed red hot. To save having to take the ashes outside they found a convenient hole in the floor boards under the tin sheet in front of the stove, it was a wonder it never set on fire. Some nights they had to find their way to Milford on exercise on foot across field without being seen (about eight miles). This was all without missing a day's work.

The life span of Albert Hine (he died in 1963) can be seen in the Church yard on his head stone where he and his wife are buried. A very cheerful and popular man among all the village people, he lived to the age of 70 and worked hard all around the "Village Green".

I Remember Albert Hine
Around the 1940's and 1950's

Albert was a Waggoner,
for Charlie Finnimore,
A strong and healthy man he was,
and stood at five foot four,
In his younger days it's told,
he would walk out of the hills
With a ewe under each arm,
in winters cold and chills.

He lived at Ivy Cottage,
where he grew his own tobacco,
For to keep his pipe alight,
it was not a laughing matter.
As the summer days got longer,
so pick leaves did he,
And hung then in the living room,
the ceiling could not see,

When dry and almost crisp they got,
into a draw he pressed
To keep them through the winter,
by large old chimney breast.

He rang church bells on Sundays,
with a team they were so loyal,
They practice in the mid-week night,
as if expecting royal,

He had a box, of twelve inches,
though he was in his prime,
The little man he rang the tenner,
keeping stead time.
The team with him at that time,
they are well remembered,
It written in the belfry sill,
names and bells all numbered.

All day he worked with horses,
a carting muck with two,
He had the one up in traces,
as the load was from the Yews,
Up to the Noons Birch field,
where he hooked it out in rucks,
Ten paces up, ten paces wide,
so even was the muck.

Describe the man were looking at,
a jerkin he did ware,
Tied round the middle with binder
twine, to hold more than just a tare,
Corduroy trousers tucked in spats,
round his hob nail boots,
Cap raked left and pipe raked right,
pouch and matches in a box.

His old waist coat worn and taty,
kept his big watch n matches dry,
The shirt it had few buttons ,
and the collar he kept it by,

For high days and holidays,
when everything was clean,
And home guard duty, when
the sergeant, he was very mean.

His platoon was made up of men,
who worked around the farms,
They mustered in the village hall,
to train as fighting men at arms,
The pork and bacon beef and taters,
butter eggs and creme,
All of these were traded,
mongst the brave old fighting men.

Albert kept his pipe and bacca,
it was woodbines for the rest,
As the smoke it was so dense,
no room for enemy they jest
This ploy worked well , no men got
lost, and warmer they could keep,
Til sergeant came and caught them,
so loaded up his jeep.

Two cows he kept and young stock,
and a few old tatty hens,
The fields where he kept them,
had sheds and tidy pens,
He mowed along the grass verge,
all the way to Stafford,
To make his hay to keep them,
and drew water from the ford.

All his life he worked dammed hard,
but slower he did get
Albert met his maker,
he was one you can't forget,

Popular and cheerful,
he lived to seven, tee
Buried in Seighford church yard ,
remembered by me and thee.

If there is no gardener there is no garden
--Stephen Covy

Chapter 29

Mothers Traditional Christmas Puddings

*We all had a stir, with the wooden spoon,
and to make a wish,
Four silver thrupeny pieces added,
one to each basin we'd pitch.*

Now on 30 November it is Advent Sunday, and it's before this date is when you are meant to make your traditional Christmas puddings.

At home when we were kids we all helped on the mixing of all the ingredients including the insertion of the silver thrupenny piece into each pudding basin, then we knew they were actually in each of the puddings that were made. All four were steamed in the old Birco electric boiler before storing on the top shelf in the pantry till Christmas.

It encouraged us to eat the pudding at Christmas time always hoping to be the one that finds the coin, but alas at times it got swallowed accidentally. Mother never lost any, she watched carefully the following day, and the coin was recovered. I don't know how many times those coins had been through our guts, but they were recycled and used the following year no matter what.

Our puddings would be double the size in this picture, rarely did it ever have time to put holly on top, and it was deemed to be too dangerous to fire with four young lads to keep an eye on, and a waste of good brandy.

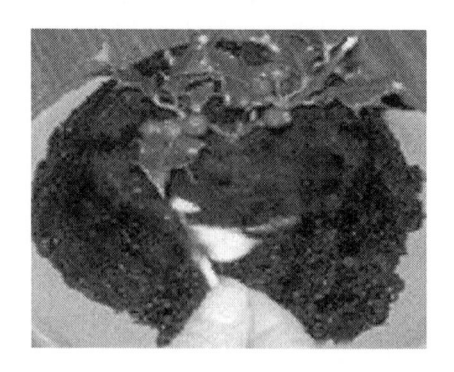

Mothers Christmas Puddings

Mother made her Christmas puddings,
well before Advent,
Got to be stored and maturing,
a month or more to ferment,
All the ingredients were ready,
along the pantry shelves,
Big bowl for mixing fetches out,
for a wooden spoon she delves.

Raisins, currants, sultanas,
beef suet, sugar and flour,
Nuts, eggs, lemon juice n' peel,
stale bread too hard to devour
Then to the bottles,
Guinness and the Brandy,
A mixture of spices, everything's
on the table ready and handy.

Thirteen ingredients there is said to be,
to mix all in the bowl
To fill four big basins, keep us going
till New Year was her goal
We all had a stir, with the wooden spoon,
and to make a wish,
Four silver thrupeny pieces added,
one to each basin she'd pitch.

Puddings tied down with a cloth,
corners pulled up tied on top,
Steamed for a good two hours,
stored on top shelf she'd pop,
Cool it was would store for months,
in fact its only one,
Exiting it was to see who,
gets the thrupeny piece be-gum.

The thrupeny pieces mother kept,
safe from year to year,
Same ones boiled every time,
occasionally swallowed I fear,
She watched so closely following day,
lose them she would not,
These were rare when we were kids,
and dug it out the pot.

It had been a long tradition,
for these puddings that she makes,
Made them every year the same,
not long does it take,
Save one for Easter time,
another special day,
See who's got the thrupeny piece,
the one who shouts hooray.

Part of the secret of success of life is to eat what you like and let the food fight it out inside.
Mark Twain (1835-1910)

Chapter 30

Corn Harvest 1940's

When father came to Seighford,
he grew a lot of wheat,
He built it into corn ricks,
along the stack yard neat,

The main cash crop apart from sugar beet, was wheat this was sown usually after a break crop of grass as in the Norfolk four coarse rotation of Roots Barley Seeds Wheat. Before sprays were brought out it was always important to give the ground a rest of perhaps 3 years of grass, to break the cycle of annual weeds, the only troublesome weeds were docks and thistles, which were pulled or spudded in the growing crop.

Wheat is sown in the autumn, then when ripe cut with a binder during August, the shoffs of wheat are then stooked in the field and left for 2 church bells (ten to fourteen days) before being carted in to the barn. It was our first real driving job in the school holidays to drive the Fordson tractor pulling the binder with father at the controls to adjust the binder according to the crop.

In the days before the tractor this was a job for a team of three horses with one man in the seat of the machine and the reigns to steer the horses, the horses would be well used to the job, and walked close alongside the crop to be cut. Only at the corners they needed guidance when they had to step sideways in unison because of the long pole stretching from the machine up to their collars.

After two weeks in the stook, the shoffs of wheat are loaded onto the wagons and taken to the rickyard, where it was built into the remaining bays of the barn. The first in the bays would be the hay for winter fodder for the cows and horses, then the corn would be built into ricks in the rickyard the shape of a house with the top going up to a ridge. This was then thatched with the previous year's straw that had been saved for the job, father would go down to the Moor Cover wood to an area that was being coppiced and cut hundreds of thatching pegs. A lot could be saved from the previous year and reused so it was a matter of topping up the number you were short.

The straw was then straightened and taken onto the roof of the stack and pegged down with string between pegs to stop it being blown away, starting round the eaves the next layer overlapping the lower one until he reached the top of the ridge. This would keep the stack dry until the threshing machine came sometime during the winter.

The threshing was done by a contractor who had a complete threshing set, of box baler and binder, pulled in the earlier days by a steam engine then latterly by a single cylinder Marshall Tractor which was more maneuverable and a lot smaller than the steamer.

I Remember Father showed us how to Thatch

When father came to Seighford,
he grew a lot of wheat,
He built it into corn ricks,
along the stack yard neat,
Started at bottom,
getting wider up to eves,
Then narrow off to great tall point,
all built out of sheaves

Then before it rained,
he would have to get it thatched,
Gathering the thatch pegs,
the thatch to rick attach,
With big long thatching ladder,
which the wheelwright made,
He took bundles of straw up top,
never he afraid.

He wound ten first pegs as bobbins,
with forty feet of twine,
Then started at the gable end,
first thatch was pegged in line,
On two feet up the ladder,
the straw he overlapped,
The twine was tight from peg to peg,
into rick were tapped.

The ladder rolled twice along the roof,
two more pegs allow,
And on again until complete,
to thatch he showed us how,
The eves were trimmed with shears,
and sides of rick also,
To give a weatherproof stack,
the result of reap and mow.

Two men travelled from farm to farm in sequence with the machinery going round the local area about once every two months. Once in the village he called at all the farms that needed corn or straw for the cattle, it took a gang of nine men to operate, that meant one man from every farm would follow it all through the village.

The driver of the steam engine would arrive from Woodseaves on his bicycle (about six miles) at six am to get steam up ready for an eight thirty start, he would stay with the steamer all day and oiling moving parts and bearing on the equipment it was driving and feeding its fire with coal. Two men would be pitching the shoffs of corn onto the thrashing box, it was an easy job throwing down from the top of the stack until lunch time, then hard work getting harder till the end of the day when it was pitching from ground level.

Two more were on top of the box one cutting the strings (or bonds as they were called) and one usually the other operator feeding the crop into the drum, the grain came out of a row of chutes where two more men bagged it off weighed it if it was for sale and stitch the top of every sack, other chutes took off the light grain and one the weed seeds.

At the other end the straw emerged into either a baler if it was for stock bedding or into a binder if it is to be used for next year's thatching, this occupied another two men and with the driver that makes nine.

On moving from the village he would often be seen calling at the Hall pool to take on water for the next day's work on the next farm.

I Remember Ozzy Alcock

Ozzy Alcock drives a threshing set,
about the parishes' local,
He's well known by everyone,
steam engine blowing whistle vocal,
A cheery smile and a wave,
to us kids all standing in a row,
A second stream of smoke arose,
from his pipe it did billow.

A wiry man with a broad and bony face,
under his oily cap,
Prominent jaw bone always shut tight,
not in his nature to yap,
Very keen eye that missed nothing,
set deep under his eyebrow,
They were bushy hung over his eyes,
dust they did not allow.

His greasy cap well pulled down,
over right eye jaunty angle,
Its really is well water proofed,
not for him a spangle,
You never saw the top of his head,
could be clean and polished,
Wispy grey hair all sticking out,
comb he must have banished.

His head was forward of his shoulders,
keenly looking out,
His nobly knuckles with grip like iron,
nothing let breakout,
Fingers oily and black with coal,
never picked his nose,
Thumbs resemble Z with pressure,
to top of pipe impose.

Twist he always smoked and chewed,
and squit tobacco juice,
Scraped out the bowel of his old pipe,
black and burnt with use.
Cut the twist with his old pen knife,
then rub it in his hand,
All mixed up with oil and coal dust,
for flavor he demand.

Always cut a knob to chew,
made inside mouth and near black,
Rinse it out with brew of tea,
and eat his mid-morning snack,
He's on the move all day long,
walking round the live machines,
Arm between the belts a flapin ,
to oil an oil cap dust he cleans.

Never had his arm pulled off,
looked dam close to me,
He's done it all his life it seems,
experience on his side has he,
Couple of shovels full of coal,
to loco fire he stokes
Plume of dark smoke blows across,
water into the boiler soaks.

At the end of the working day,
steam engine quiet and hot,
A round disc just like a plate,
place up on funnel top,
Makes it safe to leave all night,
among the chaff and straw,
Easy to get lit next day,
tall chimney makes it draw.

Onto his bike he climbs with bag,
home with bearings all well-oiled,
His mate he does the same,
their clothes with dust and dirt all soiled,
They're not much cleaner the next morning,
had a shave and scraped it all off,
Start again with loaf to toast,
cheese and homemade cake all day to scoff.

Farming looks mighty easy when your plough is a pencil, and you're a thousand miles from a corn field.
Dwight D Eisenhower (1890-1969

Chapter 31

I Remember Mothers Christmas Cakes

Father always used to make,
all our Christmas toys,
Make them in his workshop,
and hid them from us boys.

In her busy schedule of work, mother always found time to make her Christmas cake, but while she was at it she always made two.

From her experience over the years, the ingredients got depleted in the mixing bowl, as four of us would be drooling and wanting a taste. When her back was turned it would be a big finger full or if we were lucky a big spoon full of mixture would go missing, and what one had the others were all the more determined to get their share. The mixing bowl was usually the big bowl off a wash stand set, where there was a big jug as well used in the days before bathrooms and wash basins. Its volume would be about three gallons, (fifteen litres if your still classed as a youngster) and it would be a good half full.

All the currant, raisins and sultanas would be put in the basin late the night before and some spirits (usually a bit of brandy but not very much as it had got to last all Christmas) would be poured over them to soak for the night. You can guess why at night. The next day the table would be cleared soon after breakfast and all the rest of the ingredients set out. Among these was black treacle and this soon had finger dipped in. But as we knew father had a forty five gallon drum of this in the shed for the cattle, we used to take the small bung out, for it to slowly ooze out enough onto our fingers before the bung was bunged back in.

As ingredient were added two or three wooden spoons were stirring and tasting all the way through, then mother doled what was left into two big cake tins lined with paper. These were then put in the oven to cook, after a while drawing them out and testing them with a metal knitting needle, if it came out clean they were done. They were then knocked out onto wire rack to cool, with quite a few burnt sultanas and currant on the outer edges just prime for pikeing, these soon got tidied up.

Just before making the marzipan the cakes were leveled up, the top sliced off to give smooth surface to ice, this again was a chance to taste the cake, and then the marzipan was rolled out and stuck on with jam. Icing was mix and slapped on the top and smoothed down the sides to the cake boards. She stood no chance to smooth it flat and posh with so many helpers, so they were dabbed and called a snow scene. On Christmas Eve she mixed a bit more icing and coloured it red and piped a wobbly Merry Christmas across the middle.

I Remember Mother's Christmas Cake ('s)

Mother made her Christmas Cake's, every year
made two,
Mixed it in a huge bowl,
with many fingers helping drew,
Into the bowl put ingredient,
measured by rule of thumb,
This all gets depleted mixing,
a sticky mess become.

Lined the tins with brown paper,
popped them in the oven,
Couple of hours a needle test,
on this she's often done

Lift them out when they're
cooked; bump them out the tin,
Set them on a cooling rack,
dark and rich within.

Us kids were so impatient,
to taste one when it's cooled,
Usually it was following day,
four of us round it drooled,
This is why she'd made two,
got to keep abreast,
Hid the other, we never knew
where, it had got to 'rest'.

Brought it out Christmas Eve,
to marzipan and rough ice,
No use doing it sooner,
about the house are four big mice,
Snow scene's what she called it,
a snow man on the top,
Greetings n' Merry Xmas,
wobbly writing she would pop.

At tea time Christmas day,
it would suddenly appear,
Gasps of delight from us,
when she cut it we would cheer,
No more could we take,
full of turkey, trifle and mince pies,
So cake it lasted longer
aall -- over -- at -- last she sighs.

Father always liked to do a bit of carpentry, and had
his tools and workshop in a loft; one of his achievements

was a trailer to go behind his Austin car. The different people who saw this in the making were sniggering behind his back thinking he would never get it out of the door. But this was carefully thought out in his drawings on a piece of cardboard. The axle and wheels and mud guards (fenders to them who live a long way off our shores) were all removed and squeeze out onto the yard. It was designed to take pigs and sheep to market, and also to deliver potatoes, round to customers in town.

The trailer lasted about three cars, all second hand cars, but they did a lot of rough work, particularly when we were all in it at the same time. However on the months running up to Christmas he kept his workshop closed and he went working in there at nights, making toys for Father Christmas to deliver on Christmas Eve

I Remember Father made Toys for Christmas

Father always used to make,
all our Christmas toys,
Make them in his workshop,
and hid them from us boys,
Made them out of bits of wood ,
laying about the farm,
On a big flat piece of ply,
that was for the yard and barn.

Walls and gates and hedges,
painted bit of wood they were,
That was all we needed now,
so we could fields alter,
A couple of cows some sheep
and pigs and hens,
Mother had to buy these,
he made them little pens.

Saw and chop and whittle a log,
till tractor it took form,
Fix on wheels saved for this,
painted colour that was norm,
Drawbar on the back as well,
a trailer it to pull,
That he'd made a matching set,
hiding place was full.

Sometimes they were too big,
had to keep outside,
Trolleys with old pram wheels,
all of us could ride,
Someone had to push of course,
unless we found a bank,
Seating it was a little crude,
it was just a nice smooth plank.

The toys he made were very strong,
and a long time lasted,
Each of us we played ,
till next younger one he wanted,
His turn to help to ware it out,
and pass it on again,
Then it was the turn of wood
worm, chew to dust the frame.

If you can give your son or daughter only one gift, let it be enthusiasm.
Bruce Barton

Chapter 32

Animals in our Lives

Off to the vet for stitching,
twas young vet with a tutor,
But while he's knocked out,
we got the vet to neuter,

Millie the Jack Russell and Tinny the Cat

Is it any wonder that we are dominated by our animals (and kids). When you're stuck with an instinct to protect everything in our charge, they come first, come what may.

Take our little dog Millie, she is a Jack Russell, she is not allowed to be "home alone". When her principle carer goes out (my misses) she will instantly bring me (Fred) up to the top of her "pecking" order. She will follow me about the house, and settle in the next chair, and sometimes settle on the office desk.

The slightest hint that her principle carer is back and I am relegated to Zero. Only one look at the cupboard and she gets fed, whereas, I can look at the cupboard and I still have to wait until meal times. Millie should be fed dog food once a day as she does nothing, in fact she is fed at our meal times and three times in between as well (or so it seems) .The dog food is rejected in favour of best sirloin, breast of chicken, and fish but not the batter. The belly fill cereals are way down her list of options as food.

When Millie needed an operation (woman's problem you see) there was no stress on Millie on the run up to the big snip, but my misses was not to be told until the night before. Millie had a good night's sleep but her principle carer and I had a very restless night with the misses worrying about the impending op. Morning came with Millie not to have food that morning at all, in fact out of loyalty and gilt her principle carer could not eat either.

We are not talking about a normal human being but a mere DOG, Millie, the one with no tail, unless you look closely. On with her heavy collar and robust dog lead (no escape for her) into the car and off I go to do the dirty deed, among stifled tears and fond fair wells (my god she's only going for four hours).

No wonder I get rejected by most of the pets, it is always me who gets landed with the job of injecting them, or taking them to the vet where they almost invariably get injected as well. Ear drop jobs and nail clipping are other detestable jobs that I am involved in, no wonder she sees me as an expendable friend.

Later that day I picked a bleary eyed Millie up expecting at least twenty stitches and a good four inch knife hole (like her carer had). But no, we put our glasses on to look closely and mistook her op wound for her belly button, it was one miserable stitch (two when the vet took them out). Key whole surgery you see.

This is Millie, as you see she is diplomatically reads the right papers, (SOLUTIONS FOR AN UPHILL HARVEST). Should not really be on the table, but as you can see from the paws and the long claws she does not go out round the farmyard nowadays.

She is not too keen on the cats and sometimes backs off with a bloody nose, where each cat claw has penetrated a little bubble of blood pops up, and she is not too pleased.

Millie is our little dog

Millie is our little dog,
Jack Russell she is by breed,
Getting older now,
and lot of exercise does not need,
But food she loves,
and eats quite well
N' put on weight,
her tummy to swell

In her own dish bran is added,
it is for every meal,
This to help her keep regular,
but cat food tries to steal,
Sours her tummy, makes it gurgle,
make an awful noise,
Then eating grass to cure it,
and then back in play with toys.

Of people she is choosey,
the friends she has to make,
Will nip and pull ya trouser leg,
outside you must take,
She knows when we're read
go out, cower top of the stairs,
Have to go up fetch her down,
sit in kitchen mid evil glares.

Pleased to see us when we come
home, first we hear a bark,
Only half an inch of tail,
wags her bum, swings it in an arc,
Races round the kitchen floor,
dives into her bean bag,
Settles down with a new toy,
chews it to a rag.

Getting grey and older now,
knows everything you say,
Even gets on with the cat,
and even tries to play,
A touch of noses when they meet,
sometime a nip of tail,
But on the whole they're good
pals, in their holy grail.

This is to introduce Tinny (the cat)

The cats in our house only catch for sport, and that happens about once a week. Tinny, the currant beneficiary of our principle carers care, exploits this to the full. It's taken him all of six months to twig on to the system that lets him eat his belly full BEFORE going out on patrol, then strolled about the stack yard for half an hour and back to the house.

We first noticed "Tinny" (as a stray cat) on the lawn one morning when we were having coffee. He had a humped back and squatting against the wall with his head down, and we thought it was a large stone. Then it moved, and realized it was a cat. We rushed out thinking he was injured, but no, he had his head jammed inside of a ring pull dog food can. Thinking it might be a wild or nervous cat, we lifted him up by the can thinking he would drop out, but it was tight. To make any progress without injuring him, I had to pinch and pull the hair behind each ear a bit at a time until both ears popped out, then the can dropped off, or should I say he dropped out of the can. He was very dazed because he could hardly breathe, and obviously hungry, that was the reason for getting his head trapped.

When he started on our carers care, he would eat anything offered to him, and he was fed in the shed for at least two days, then he became conscious enough to know where it was coming from. This was when he was called Tinny, and was put on a "build me up diet", which included being wormed. After a few weeks we noticed he was licking a patch on his fur partway up his back leg, and on investigation found it was a cut.

When the fur was parted it opened into a round hole that you could put your finger in. It had to be stitched so we made an appointment for him at the vets, and they were instructed while they had him to knock his tabs off at the same time. This cost me a princely sum of fifty quid plus vat, all for a stray cat called Tinny.

At this point in time he became house bound and has never got out of the habit. From time to time he goes on patrol and catches only the smallest of rats for a bit of sport, but the small ones would eventually become big ones so he is forgiven.

This is where Tinny sits in the morning sun, he is far from a posh cat, and he is a happy cat. Never outside for more than half has an hour twice a day, so when are you planting out the bedding plants it advisable to be had wearing gloved.

About twelve weeks ago he got very miserable and was losing weight to the point we had to take him to the vets. It was found that he had got some bad teeth, so he was put under and the offending teeth removed. We were shocked to find when we got him home we looked in his mouth to find over half his teeth had gone, so now he does not have any dry cat biscuits, and the odd bit of meat he gums it to death, and keeps him happy for ages, he has also put his weight back on as well.

A Cat Called Tinny

We found a cat upon the lawn;
his head was in a tin,
A tin that had a raged edge,
and should be in the bin,
This hungry cat to reach a lick,
of food that's in the bottom,
Shoved his head in over his ears,
to get out was his problem.

He'd reversed around the lawn
all night, in a bit of bother,
Sat there with his back humped up,
he thought he was a goner,
Picked up the tin for him drop out,
but firmly was he wedged,
So tight around his head it was,
to his maker he was pledged.

To breath it was a problem,
suffocation he just missed,
Pulled the hair behind his ears,
to extract his head insist,
Found one ear and then the other,
and out the tin he popped,
Lay there dopy in a daze,
and stay exactly where he dropped.

Resuscitation's what he wanted,
and he got it in the house,
This hungry cat around the yard,
could not find his mouse,
A little bit of tender care,
and food to fill his belly,
Day or two it was before,
went out with legs like jelly.

So vulnerable was this cat right now,
new home he had found,
And in the following weeks,
found strength to trot around,
Into trouble again he was,
an injury to his knee,
A hole in his flesh as though,
was there to take a key.

Off to the vet for stitching,
twas young vet with a tutor,
But while he's knocked out,
we got the vet to neuter,
Two lots of stitches made him sway,
but stronger did he get,
Hardly leaves the house at all,
so lazy is this cat you bet.

Comforts what he yearns for,
and its comfort what he's got,
So a name is what he's short of,
one that's relevant to his lot,
'Canny' doesn't sound right,
then Tinny' came to mind,
'Tinny's' what he's called now,
now he's safe and sound.

I like pigs. Dogs look up to us. Cats look down on us. Pigs treat us as equals.
Sir Winston Churchill (1847 – 1965)

The old Yews Farm yard in the 1950's

A patchwork quilt.
To give you an idea of where in Seighford it is, -- Top left is Clanford Hall. Bottom right is Aston Hall.

This book continues in
The Longest Swath Volume 2

It includes more old characters of the village, our woodwork teacher at school, and our family tree.

Gardening, moles, worms, a visit to the seaside, water meadows, the village pump, and home guard Contraband and many other tales.

Printed in Great Britain
by Amazon